WHAT
CHRISTIANS
BELIEVE

WHAT
CHRISTIANS
BELIEVE

David Craig

ONEWORLD

OXFORD

For Andrew, Angus and Elizabeth with love

WHAT CHRISTIANS BELIEVE

Oneworld Publications
(Sales and Editorial)
185 Banbury Road
Oxford OX2 7AR
England
http://www.oneworld–publications.com

Oneworld Publications
(US Marketing Office)
160 N Washington St.
4th Floor, Boston
MA 02114
USA

© David Craig 2000

All rights reserved.
Copyright under Berne Convention
A CIP record for this book is available
from the British Library

ISBN 1–85168–218–X

Cover design by Design Deluxe
Typeset by Saxon Graphics Ltd, Derby
Printed in England by Clays Ltd, St Ives plc

Contents

The Apostles' Creed

I believe in God the Father almighty
Maker of heaven and earth,
And in Jesus Christ his only Son our Lord
Who was conceived by the Holy Ghost
Born of the Virgin Mary
Suffered under Pontius Pilate
Was crucified, dead and buried.
He descended into Hell.
The third day he rose again from the dead.
He ascended into Heaven
And sitteth on the Right hand of God the Father.
From thence he shall come to judge the quick and the dead.
I believe in the Holy Ghost,
The Holy Catholic Church,
The Communion of Saints,
The Forgiveness of sins,
The Resurrection of the body,
And the life everlasting.

Introduction

Any attempt to condense what it is that Christians believe into the compass of a few pages – the equivalent of three hours of broadcasting – is to offer oneself up to accusations of naive simplification, of super-ficiality, of arrogance, as well as to a whole host of other sins of omission! Each would be right: but broadcasters live in a world of limitations: of budget, of editorial control and above all of time. In almost twenty years of programme-making, how often has appeal been made to a Network Controller that a series would be much better were it to be twice or three times as long, with ten or fifteen parts rather than five, and that each programme should be of forty-five rather than thirty minutes!

To provide an audience as wide as that of the BBC World Service with an introduction to the basic tenets of Christian belief in three hours is a tall order, but no taller than providing a similar audience with introductions to Islam, Judaism, Hinduism and Buddhism – all series which have been made in the past few years – and which have also been published in book form, thanks to Oneworld. The challenges remain the same. How can you explain in simple language and in such limited space what generations of academics, practitioners and spiritually-enlightened devotees have taken centuries to define, refine and experience?

It would be relatively easy to produce an academic, credally-based series which compared orthodox with heretical dogma, traditional with modernist practice, liturgical variations, indigenous and dias-poric religion. At another level it would be relatively simple to produce an experiential series dependent upon testimony and personal experiences of a religion. The difficulty comes in finding a way of expressing that combination of theological and dogmatic with the personal and practical which is the nature of any living religion.

What Do Christians Believe? started from the simple structure of one of the earliest statements of Christian belief, the Apostles' Creed. It was modified by the need to combine theological accuracy with practical manifestation, and changed because the sources were contemporary practitioners. In broadcasting there are no footnotes, no bibliographies, no appendices: what you hear is what you get, and unlike a book there is no chance to go back to a section that was not immediately accessible on the first reading and reread it, looking up unfamiliar words and concepts in lexicons and theological dictionaries. Like the Atonement in Christian theology, a broadcast is 'once and for all'.

At one level a broadcast programme is not unlike an anthology in that it is formed by a collection of contributors, people who on some occasions represent an establishment position and reflect the considered authority of a specific tradition, and others who 'speak for themselves'. What they have to say alters any preconceived treatment, shapes the argument and dictates what line of discussion the programme will take. Sometimes a single contribution causes the editor to recast an entire series. But at another level it is the editor who ultimately selects for inclusion those parts of the various contributions which have been offered by interviewees. However, much relevant material that has to be rejected from programmes can be recovered and included in a book, so the written account is inevitably expanded. Inflection conveys much that the written word cannot, and so elements of colour have been added to provide background and authenticity. It is said that radio has much better pictures than television because they are in the listener's mind, they challenge the imagination. In the book, a picture needs to be described, atmosphere spelt out and inflection interpreted.

There is no doubt that the tenets of Christian belief are universal, but the founder of the faith lived in a specific geographical location, at a set point in history. It is impossible to understand the significance of

Jesus without some reference to the land in which he lived, the land where placenames resonate with the journeyings of Abraham and the patriarchs, the tribal divisions, the civilizing work of the judges, the uniting force of the kings and, once a kingdom, the inevitable conflicts with neighbouring powers: Syrian, Babylonian and Hellenic cultures, and finally the all-conquering power of the Roman Empire. This is the archaeological and religious palimpsest over which the life of Jesus was written. More books have been written about Jesus than about any other figure. There are endless specialist treatments of historical and cultural backgrounds or contemporary theological influences which may have influenced or even provoked the ministry of Jesus: did he come from a Pharisaic, Sadducean or Essene background? Was he a poor jobbing carpenter, or did his father, Joseph, have a profitable business in this far-away province of the Roman Empire? Was he a revolutionary seeking to overthrow the Roman Empire? Did he start a new religion or was he just the latest in a long line of Jewish teachers who had reformed and changed the religion of Moses? How did his teaching influence other religions?

While acknowledging the libraries of books about Jesus, it is also important to note that the primary sources for the life of Jesus are found in the New Testament, and particularly in the first four books: the gospels according to Matthew, Mark, Luke and John. Each is a remarkably short biography written from a different perspective, at a slightly different time, with a different audience in mind. Matthew depends for much of his material on Mark's gospel (as indeed does Luke), and his account is dated by scholars as having been written between 80 and 90 CE, some fifty to sixty years after the events it describes. Matthew writes for a predominantly Jewish audience and is concerned throughout his gospel to identify Jesus as the expected Messiah. He frequently describes events in scriptural terms as fulfilling the prophecies associated with the Messiah.

Mark, considered to be the first gospel written, is the shortest, with a terse narrative where events fall over each other and are compressed. The author can't wait to tell his story, and event after event follow with the phrases 'and then', or 'next', or 'straightway'.

His Greek is the least stylized, representing the *lingua franca* of the area. Papias, a Bishop of Hierapolis who lived from *c.* 60–130 CE, states (on the authority of John the Presbyter, the purported author of the Letters of John found at the end of the New Testament) that Mark, having become the interpreter of St Peter, set down 'accurately everything he remembered of the words and actions of the Lord'. Again, from internal evidence, scholars date his collection of stories from the death of Peter in 64 CE.

Luke is not only the author of the third gospel; he is also the author of the Acts of the Apostles to which readers can turn for further information about the influence of the life of Jesus and also for the earliest history of the growth of the Christian religion and the establishment of small Christian communities throughout Europe and Asia Minor. The gospel of Luke, written in the most elegant of Greek styles, could well have been designed for a non-Christian readership: his material portrays the Roman authorities in the most favourable light, and he is at pains to place particular events in an international historical perspective: for example, it is from his gospel that we learn that the birth of Jesus took place at the time of the census when Quirinius was governor of Judea, which we can date as 6 CE. Scholars are inclined to dismiss this as a mistake and argue for a birth date some eight or nine years earlier.

These first three gospels have much in common: they recount in narrative form the birth and early life of Jesus, but then there is a gap of some twenty years until, in a burst of activity, he emerges into the public eye in a series of events that turned the contemporary Jewish world upside down. He is baptized in the river Jordan by his cousin John, he preaches in such a way that his audiences have to rethink what it means to be Jewish and religious. He preaches 'with authority and not as the scribes and Pharisees', the traditional interpreters of Jewish law and custom. He performs wonders (a later gospel, John's, calls them 'signs') indicative of the greatness of God, and claims that it is not he who is accomplishing these actions but God working through him. He teaches in traditional rabbinic manner, exchanging question for question, using illustrations that his listeners would be familiar with from personal experience: the marketplace, the farmyard, the buying and selling of small commercial enterprises and, a significant perspective, the obviously straitened circumstances of a people occupied by a foreign power, struggling to pay taxes, educate and feed families and maintain their religious identity.

The fourth gospel is significantly different, in that it is at pains to point out the theological significance of Jesus' ministry and words: for this author it is the significance of events rather than events themselves which are important. Above all, John identifies Jesus as the eternal Son of God, pre-existent before the creation of the world and, as such, an integral part of God's design and purpose. In John 'the Word became flesh' and with Jesus, God's purpose intended from the beginning of the world is affirmed. Obviously John is a later gospel written not by an eye-witness but a commentator who includes material from other sources for his story-line and goes on to illuminate them with his own Christological understandings and interpretations.

It has often been said that a return to the text of the Bible can wonderfully illuminate the work of the commentators, and in this book I make no apology for returning time and time again to the source book of the Christian faith. That collection of documents, together with the land on which Jesus walked, is what has influenced generations of believers and is what informs and influences the people who took part in the programmes, and whose contributions make the major part of this book.

But first let us consider what this book is *not*! It is, first of all, *not* a comprehensive survey of contemporary Christian theology. It is *not* a chronological account of Christian doctrines. There is no mention of the deciding moments of Christian doctrine, no councils, no creeds and few controversies. There are no references to heresies, to accounts of persecutions or inquisitions, to reformations or counter-reformations. There is very little reference to the churchmanship of various contributors. Orthodox, Catholic and Protestant traditions are seldom mentioned and their differences are rarely at issue. There is no attempt to follow the development of particular beliefs or to analyse ways in which different branches of the church have provided their identities by highlighting particular doctrines.

3 1326 00315 2594

By interviewing a number of Christians, academics and practitioners, men and women, ordained and lay, we have tried to find out how belief in particular elements of the Christian faith came about, where they came from and how they have influenced the living and thinking of some contemporary practitioners.

For Christians, it is the pictures of the Incarnation – the Word made flesh – that provide occasions of liturgical celebration: for example, the Annunciation of the birth of Jesus to Mary by an angel, the birth of the Messiah at Christmas, the revelation of his status at the Epiphany. These moments of liturgical and congregational joy are thrown into dramatic perspective by the pictures of alienation, exclusion and execution which describe the final days of the life of Jesus, and which in turn are marked by the most powerful of Christian liturgies. It would be hard for a Christian to celebrate Christmas or commemorate Holy Week without liturgical acts or in isolation from others. But for Christians, to limit these events in the life of Jesus to activities associated exclusively with churchgoing would be to ignore much of what it means to live life as a Christian.

It is easy to know *about* a religion: there are enough books which describe its doctrine, history and liturgical celebrations, its statistics, demography and social breakdown. It is relatively easy to write about such phenomena or even to make programmes about them! It is not so easy to know what it means to be a practising member of that religion. This is what the series *What Do Christians Believe?* attempted to do. This is what this book attempts to do.

The following pages are an account of the process, and it must be left to the listener – or in this case the reader – to decide whether we succeed or not! It is fair to say that the editor of a series often possesses the tenacity of a terrier dog, encouraging and criticizing the presenter's progress, overseeing the interviews and ultimately deciding what is included. Much of the creativity of a series comes from the presentation of the programmes: the style of engagement, the idiosyncratic touch and the interaction with so many of the contacts. *What Do Christians Believe?* is no different. Alison Hilliard interviewed, listened to tapes, selected major extracts for inclusion in the series and ultimately gave each programme its distinctive style. These chapters build on her work, expanding some of the issues and including material for which the unyielding strictures of a thirty-minute broadcast allowed no time!

A NOTE ABOUT THE CONVENTIONS USED

Throughout, the terms Common Era (CE) and Before the Common Era (BCE) have been used rather than the more traditional AD and BC: perhaps in a book about Christian faith this may seem provocative but in a new millennium there is serious justification for this convention. While in the West fewer people may claim to be practising Christians, all acknowledge that they live in a society whose cultural inheritance is Christian and whose social organization is based upon Christian initiatives. But to those who find this convention an abrogation of Christian imperatives, I apologize!

All quotations come from the Revised Standard Version of the Bible, the edition I personally prefer for its simplicity, exact translation and the familiarity of its language. There are many translations available, newer, more immediate but in many cases ephemeral. To have chosen one of these would have been to exclude others. The RSV will, I suspect, be with us long after many of the newer translations are left to gather dust on bookshelves. Finally I have included some authoritative definitions to provide some structure for the comments of individual contributors.

1

God the Father Almighty, Maker of Heaven and Earth

In the beginning God created the heavens and the earth. The earth was without form and void, and darkness was upon the face of the deep; and the Spirit of God was moving over the face of the waters. And God said, 'Let there be light'; and there was light. And God saw that the light was good; and God separated the light from the darkness. God called the light Day, and the darkness he called Night. And there was evening and there was morning, one day.

Genesis 1:1–5

So begins the first book of the Bible. It recounts how in six days God created the heavens and the earth and all that is in them: and how, on the seventh day, he rested.

Each culture has its own creation story distilled from different local oral traditions. Each attempts to provide an account for the origins and location of a society, its practices and its relationship with its creator. Each religion has its own cosmology which gives accounts of the origin and nature of the universe but – in the case of Genesis – in such a way as to show the world as a place of opportunity for God's action. Because of this specific purpose, religions frequently offer different, sometimes conflicting, cosmologies without much attempt to reconcile the differences between them. The Jewish scriptures have at least six different creation narratives which are integrated to provide the origins for the religion of Yahweh, Judaism.

Western Christian tradition has long regarded the creation story of the first chapter of Genesis as one of the great stories which developed in what is now eurocentrically called the Middle East. It belonged, along with the Epic of Gilgamesh, to a series of similar stories which set out to explain the existence of the world as we know it, and it is one of a number of stories which have been gathered together by the various editors in the book of Genesis.

However, in the United States of America today, up to fifty per cent of American Christians would claim to accept this account as true and literal fact. They call themselves Creationists.

Based in a desert valley in Southern California, *The Institute for Creation Research* was established in 1972 as one of a number of related organizations set up to defend the biblical account of creation against what its founders saw as the mistaken and immoral teachings of evolution, which argue as the result of scientific observation and research, that the universe and all things in it are the result of a long evolutionary process. Modern-day Creationists are the direct successors of American fundamentalists such as William Jennings Bryan who, after the First World War, pressed to ban the teaching of biological evolution in schools, and George McCready Price, who searched for scientific evidence for a young earth and a worldwide flood.

The Institute runs its own radio station, *Science Creation Radio,* which broadcasts radio programmes such as *Scripture, Science and Salvation* every week throughout the United States. Through its publications, broadcasts and projects, *The Institute for Creation Research* attempts to rebut the accusation that Creationism is based solely on a religious bias and which identifies Creationism as a 'phenomenon that can be cured by better education'. It is the largest such organization in the world, providing seminars, courses and opportunities for research. Dr Larry Vardmann teaches graduate programmes at the Institute:

> We are trying to revive a theistic basis for science. We are trying to show that a biblical model of earth history and processes is a valid perspective, and that is why this is the Centre for creation research.

We're not just taking the Bible and espousing it, we're doing science research in order to be able to demonstrate that some of the concepts we have can be supported from scientific investigation as well as a biblical perspective.

It should be recorded that although the Creation Research Society supports the publication of creation science papers, these documents have not been recognized as serious science by any academics outside the movement.

Members of the Institute are all young-earth Creationists who hold that God created the world not more than ten thousand years ago and in six days, just as recorded in the book of Genesis. They reject the theory of evolution as developed by Charles Darwin and published in 1859 in *The Origin of Species*. His argument – that the earth and its millions of species evolved over billions of years by natural selection – is supported by the majority of scientists, but Creationists raise objections to neo-Darwinian theory, citing gaps in the fossil record or the absence of interim forms in the production of complex organisms or organs.

For Bill Hash, the Institute's Public Information Officer, faith is dependent upon the literal accuracy of the creation stories in Genesis.

Personally, as a Christian, I trust in certain facts of history as true: I believe there is a God who is real and who did create, as Genesis says, in the beginning. If science did really overthrow the fact that God did create as a matter of history, I would throw my Bible out of the window, because I don't think it holds up. My faith is only good so long as certain facts are true.

In addition to its teaching and publishing programme, the Institute also runs a museum of creation history and earth history. The exhibits are laid out in rooms corresponding to the six days of creation, and include a model reconstruction of Noah's ark and displays of the ice age and fossils – seen as a direct result of the flood. Visitors, many of them children who are taught Creationism in Christian schools in America, are impressed. As they inspected the museum these comments, overheard in the galleries, reflected their Creationist education and background:

I believe the Creationist point of view is more logical...

It is pretty obvious that evolution is not right and Creationism is better...

I think evolution is not sure any more...

If we came from apes we are not worth anything...

I believe that creation happened in six days, and I think it is hard to believe in evolution and that everything happened just by chance.

But according to Bishop Jack Spong, the Episcopal Bishop of Newark and one of the most outspoken liberal bishops in America, these young people are treading in dangerous water:

My feeling is that if the biblical account of creation and the literalized form is the cornerstone of anyone's faith they are going to be totally disillusioned. The thought of Charles Darwin and the whole field of evolution has captured the world. It is not a theory. Even the Vatican in 1995 acknowledged that Darwin was correct. Every biological textbook, medical science, organ transplants, and transplants where animal organs are used in human surgical procedures, assumes the truth of Darwin. So if anyone assumes the old creation story is a true story they are dancing to a tune that is no longer being played, and that is a cruel delusion.

Mainstream academic theologians like Professor Keith Ward, the Regius Professor of Divinity at the University of Oxford, also warn against taking the creation story literally. He believes that to argue about what happened when is to misunderstand the significance of what creation really means:

Creation means that the whole of the universe at every point of time – including now – depends entirely upon God and upon nothing else for its existence. So what creation means is that the whole universe depends upon God and that God wants the universe to exist. It really has nothing to do with whether or not the universe began. It is just a misunderstanding for people to think that creation is the first moment of the universe and that then God went to sleep perhaps and let it go on along its own way. Creation has to be dependent upon God every moment of the time. If people considered this, looked at creation in this context, then they would perhaps be less bothered about whether the account of creation in the book of Genesis was correct or not, or whether it was literal or not.

The Jewish prayer book describes God as 'he who renews the work of creation every day'. The *Book of Common Prayer* of the Church of England invites Christians, in the prayer called *The General Thanksgiving*, to 'give thanks for our creation, preservation and all the blessings of this life' identifying creation with preservation. If God were to withdraw his continuing act of creativity, then all things would cease to exist.

But with the very first word of the Bible a problem can be identified. If you interpret accurately the opening word of the Bible, *Bereshith* in Hebrew, it must be translated not just 'in the beginning' but *'in the beginning of'* where *reshith* means start or beginning in the construct state and the *be* the preposition 'in' or 'at'. However in Proverbs 8, the word *reshith* is found describing Wisdom, and so the opening of the creation story could be translated 'by means of Wisdom, God created' a concept which gives a certain coherence to one of the roles attributed to Jesus.

While Christians obviously inherited the Jewish creation stories and a common Semitic cosmology, they have always associated Jesus with the activity of the Father in creation.

> *Yet for us there is one God, the Father, from whom are all things and for whom we exist, and one Lord, Jesus Christ, through whom are all things and through whom we exist.* (1 Cor. 8:6)

> *He is the image of the invisible God, the first-born of all creation; for in him all things were created, in heaven and on earth, visible and invisible, whether thrones or dominions or principalities or authorities – all things were created through him and for him. He is before all things, and in him all things hold together.* (Col. 1:15–17)

But to talk of a single account of creation in the book of Genesis would be to simplify the texts, as the different types of creation narrative in the Jewish scriptures are told from the perspectives of different people who believed in the cult of Yahweh. They represented groups as diverse as a farming community, a priestly hierarchy, wise men and prophets; there are stories told from cultic and from apocalyptic perspectives, but they all start from the premise that the world was created solely in obedience to the divine will. Chapter 1 of Genesis is, without question, devised to reflect a priestly position. As Gerhard von Rad wrote in his commentary on Genesis:

> Whoever expounds Genesis chapter 1 must understand one thing: this chapter is Priestly doctrine – indeed it contains the essence of Priestly knowledge in a most concentrated form. It was not written 'once upon a time' but rather it is doctrine which has been carefully enriched over centuries by very slow growth. Nothing is here by chance; everything must be considered carefully, deliberately, and precisely... What is said here is intended to hold true entirely and exactly as it stands. (Gerhard von Rad, Genesis, SCM Press)

While that may be fine for theologians, for farmers and maybe prophets, how do scientists – modern-day wise men – who are Christians see the story of creation? The Revd Dr John Polkinghorne is both a priest and a theoretical physicist:

> I think people who take the literal account are unfortunate. I think they are missing the point of scripture in that they are not taking it sufficiently seriously. They are trying to treat it as if it were a substitute for science, rather than being a deep theological resource.
>
> I don't read the creation story in Genesis as an account of how things began, a blow-by-blow account of how things came to be. I don't think it is intended to provide scientific but theological information, and its main message is that nothing exists unless God wishes it to be in being.
>
> It is impossible to take it literally because there are at least two separate accounts, one in Genesis 1 which is a relatively sophisticated story and one in Genesis 2 which is the more ancient story, and they don't agree with each other. I take them as myths, by which I don't mean untruths but stories which contain deep truths. One is that the

world exists because God wills it to exist, the other which is repeated throughout the story is that God's creation is good.

Scientifically the story of the universe can be traced back to the big bang about fifteen billion years ago when the world started extremely simply as just a ball of energy. But after those fifteen billion years of evolving history it has become extremely complex, with humans being the most interesting consequences of that history known to us. That's the scientific story and I take it absolutely seriously.

I want to understand, however, why that has happened, why the world exists and why it is so fruitful, why it is so orderly. Scientists are deeply impressed with the rational beauty of the world – the order of the world. It looks like a world shot through with signs of mind and it is deeply attractive to religious believers to understand that order as the reflection of the capital 'M' of the Mind of God.

Professor Polkinghorne can reconcile the scientific development and progression with the account of creation as found in Genesis because for him it is congruent with the way the story of how things happens sits with *why* they happen.

There are two different levels of understanding about what is going on. The scientific story is a kind of causal account: this leads to that which in turn leads to the next thing. The religious story is an account of meaning – what is going on, what is the purpose that is being fulfilled, why the world exists.

Scientists like John Polkinghorne believe that both religious and scientific stories of explanation point towards belief in God:

There are always puzzles and perplexities about how the scientific view of the world and the religious view relate together but I've never faced a crisis about having to choose between the two. In fact if I am going to understand what is going on in the world, I think it needs the insights of science and the insights of religion. Together they can give me a much better understanding, a sort of two-eyed vision of the world.

I think the scientific story does contain hints that there is a divine will and purpose behind the world. One is that the world is so orderly and so beautiful. I worked as a theoretical physicist, and the search for fundamental theories in physics is the search for beautiful equations, and the experience and reward of doing physics is the sense of wonder at the beautiful structure of the world that is revealed. Now is that luck or a happy accident or is there a reflection that there is indeed a divine mind behind it all?

The second thing that has emerged from science which I think is very interesting and significant is that we have come to realize that the way life has evolved in our universe has depended very specifically on the physical fabric of the world. It is not just any old world that after fifteen billion years is capable of evolving human beings. It is a special world finely tuned in its particular laws and circumstances. There is a very real scientific sense in which the potentiality for life had to be present from the big bang onwards, and this suggests to me that this world is not just any old world but is a creation which has been endowed by its creator with just those finely tuned laws and circumstances which would give it a fruitful history.

Science tells us another thing about the history of the universe, and that is that it has been an evolving history, and evolving is an exploration and realization of that potentiality. And it does so in particular ways; it is, as people say, an interaction between chance and necessity. By necessity they mean the lawful regulation of the world and by chance they don't mean meaninglessness or a sort of cosmic lottery, but a historical contingency. And the way life has evolved certainly contains elements of historical particularity. I don't think it was laid down from the beginning that humans were going to have five fingers. So the world is in some ways free to explore, to become, to be itself, and in fact in 1859 when Darwin published The Origin of Species and the whole idea of biological evolution came on the scene, some clergymen, including Charles Kingsley, said that means an evolutionary world is a world God has created and allowed to make itself. The cosmic story is not the performance of a fixed divine script but a fruitful improvization.

But it is the origin of human beings which still taxes many Christians who generally accept the Darwinian theory of evolution. Mgr Vincent Nichols is the Roman Catholic Bishop in North London. He is uneasy identifying human beings as the product of just another stage in the earth's evolution:

> I think what Catholic faith would be most concerned to preserve is a distinctiveness in the human person which separates the human being from other parts of creation. And one aspect of that distinctiveness is that only the human being is endowed with a self-conscious spiritual capacity enabling him to enter into a relationship with God. Now I think the problem lies in answering the question, when did that emerge and how did that emerge? I do not see a totally satisfactory answer to those questions in a purely mechanistic theory of evolution – it would seem to me that there has to be a point at which a qualitative difference appears, whether by a leap or by some other intervention which marks the point at which the human person is able to receive the revelation of God and the invitation of God to a life of faith and love, of relationship with God.

But what image of God emerges from the creation story? Sister Lavinia Byrne is a theologian teaching at Cambridge, a Roman Catholic nun who, until January 2000, was a member of the Institute of the Blessed Virgin Mary:

> For a start, we are presented in the book of Genesis with the image of a male creator. It is fascinating that the maleness of God is taught in the earliest pages of the Hebrew scriptures. It must be seen against a backdrop of the other creation stories which were available at that time. In one of them the world seemed to be spawned in a kind of irresponsible way from a kind of giant earth-goddess who coupled with anyone who was around, including one of her own sons. So from that sort of story the creation of the earth and of human beings was seen as an irresponsible act; an act of desire; an act of irregular coupling.
>
> When one comes to the Hebrew scriptures, the creator God of the beginning of Genesis is one of huge consciousness and decision who says 'Let us Make'. Some of the first words of the Bible are

words of permission: 'Let us make man in our own image and likeness, male and female let us create them.'

Martin Palmer is an Anglican environmentalist who sees the story of creation as told in the Bible as a radical departure from previous cosmologies:

> What the writer of Genesis did which was so revolutionary – theologically – was that he or she took a very ancient story which had the particular message that human beings were of absolutely no significance, everything in creation was here as playthings of the gods, and what that writer of Genesis did was to take the story and turn it on its head. I am going to make the extraordinary claim that the whole of creation is actually an expression of God's love; not God's folly or anger or game-playing, but that all aspects are loved by God, and I am also going to make the claim that we human beings who have traditionally seen ourselves mythologically as of no consequence whatsoever to the gods are actually partners with God in his work of creation.

Partners with God and further, we are told in the biblical story, made in the image of God (Gen. 1:26–7). This is a claim that has puzzled Christians for centuries. Professor Keith Ward suggests that being made 'in the likeness of God' involves a conscious knowledge and love of God:

> I think one can say it certainly does not mean that human beings look like God. Because God is not material it is not physical resemblance. Most theologians now think that it means we are made for relationship with God. We are made in the image of God so that we can relate to God personally through worship and prayer and loving relationship. So in that sense human beings are special because they can have a conscious knowledge and love of God. And even though they are made of dust – and I think that is a profound insight into the human condition as revealed in the creation story – we really are parts of the material world. We have a function of relating consciously to the creator, and this is certainly part of the creation story.

According to the Hebrew scripture, being made in the image of God has specific practical implications. It means believers are commanded to walk in his ways. They are commanded to imitate God. This is how one of the early rabbis interpreted the command in his exegesis of the scriptural text:

> How can a person walk after God? What is meant is that one ought to walk after the attributes of God. Just as the Lord clothed the naked, so you shall clothe the naked. Just as he visits the sick, so you shall visit the sick. Just as he comforts mourners, so you shall comfort mourners. Just as he buries the dead so shall you bury the dead.

This is surely the inspiration for the teaching of Jesus, which takes the practical involvement even further. St Matthew recounts in his gospel chapter 25, verses 31–46 a story Jesus told to stress the importance of walking in the ways of God. On the Day of Judgement, Jesus says, the world will be divided between sheep and goats. The sheep – those who have fed the hungry, given drink to the thirsty, welcomed strangers, and visited the sick and prisoners – will inherit the Kingdom of God that had been prepared for them from the foundation of the world (in the beginning), while the goats – those who failed to acknowledge the needs of their fellow human beings – are to be cast into an eternal fire prepared by the devil and his angels. Walking after God is the hallmark of those people who have chosen life rather than death, who have become fellow-creators with God in the on-going work of creation, preservation and blessing of life.

For Christians the statement that human beings are made in the likeness of God is at the heart of their Christian faith and dictates the way they live their lives. It has practical and sometimes painful implications. Lynda Brayer is a Jew from South Africa who went to Israel to practise as a lawyer and in the 1980s converted to Christianity and was baptized a Catholic. For her the application of Israeli state law presents a professional as well as a personal challenge. She runs a legal aid centre helping those Palestinians who, as the result of Israel's strictly imposed building regulations, have had their land confiscated, been made refugees in their own land by eviction or had their homes demolished in front of their eyes, perhaps for the infringement of a legal restriction, or perhaps, as in some cases, in retribution for acts of opposition to the Israeli Defence Force.

One such case is the Abumidgemuh family – a Muslim family in East Jerusalem – whose house was demolished after being built without the necessary building permit. The fifteen members of the family at the time of writing live in Red Cross tents and two ship containers. Lynda Brayer has taken their plight to the Israeli Court. It is typical of the work she does – work she believes is inspired by the message in the creation story:

> For me that means not only am I created in God's image but so are you and so is everyone else – each and every one of us is a child of God. I think that what Jesus did when he came was to reinforce the basic idea in Genesis that we are all sacred beings and that all life is sacred. It is sacred both because God created us and also because we carry in ourselves the image of him. And that image is an image of freedom, an image of a capacity to love and an image of relationships, and so for me, in my everyday life, in my work and everything I do, I feel duty-bound to behave to everyone around me and to do my work as a lawyer for people because that is the way to serve God and to love God. It is essential to remember that, while you are doing things for people, you are obliged to treat each one of them with absolute dignity and as of ultimate worth, regardless of a person's faith, ethnic origin or gender.

The gender question in the creation stories has been a divisive issue for Christians down the centuries. For some Christians the order of creation points to an important truth. After all, the Bible narratives tell how man was created first and then woman. Lavinia Byrne argues that this has had implications for the way the church, in the form of Christian bureaucracy, has treated women:

> In the second creation narrative, which is in fact an earlier story, we are told about human beings; Adam and Eve are described as being made in one day. Adam was created first and then he was feeling

lonely, looking at the animals both male and female, giving them all names and searching around for a mate but not finding one.

Then the Lord God said, 'It is not good that the man should be alone; I will make him a helper fit for him.' So out of the ground the Lord God formed every beast of the field and every bird of the air, and brought them to the man to see what he would call them; and whatever the man called every living creature, that was its name... but for the man there was not found a helper fit for him. So the Lord God caused a deep sleep to fall upon the man, and while he slept took one of his ribs and closed up its place with flesh; and the rib which the Lord God had taken from the man he made into a woman and brought her to the man. Then the man said, 'This at last is bone of my bones and flesh of my flesh; she shall be called Woman because she was taken out of Man.' (Gen. 2:18–23)

Although it is a wonderfully moving story it is, says Lavinia Byrne, a story which implies that woman is made not *with* man but *for* man and this is a source of great trouble for contemporary women.

The story which follows tells how God puts Adam and Eve into a garden, gives them freedom to wander where they like and eat what they like from its produce with the exception of a single tree. Eve, tempted by a talking serpent to try fruit from this forbidden tree, discovers its sweetness and offers it to Adam who in turn succumbs to the temptation and eats the fruit. As a result, 'the eyes of both were opened, and they knew that they were naked; and they sewed fig leaves together and made themselves aprons.'

It is the story of original sin and, argues Lavinia Byrne, it makes the woman appear as the initiator. It is she who brings about human sin and that is why it is a story which troubles us to this day: was woman made for man or with man, was woman made as a moral equal or a source of temptation? This issue remains unresolved.

This narrative of the 'Fall' has been the source of enormous problems to women in the past. Because of this original disobedience to the command of God, humanity has been condemned to the human condition of pain, toil and mortality. In his letter to the church at Rome Paul uses this story to explain the coming into the world of sin:

> *Therefore as sin came into the world through one man and death*
> *through sin, and so death spread to all men because all men sinned –*
> *sin indeed was in the world before the law was given, but sin is not*
> *counted where there is no law.* (Rom. 5:12–13)

A broadly accepted and more modern interpretation of this Genesis story is that it is a myth to explain that sin came into the world as the result of human choice and that all human life has subsequently been transformed from what God intended into something which humanity wanted, and that something must, because it is other than what God intended, be inferior.

Original sin, according to traditional Christian theology, is that state into which every human being is born because of the fall of Adam. As a fifteenth-century poem has it:

> Adam lay y-bounden,
> Bounden in a bond;
> Four thousand winter
> Thought he not too long.
>
> And all was for an apple,
> An apple that he took,
> As clerkes finden
> Written in their book.
>
> Ne had the apple taken been,
> The apple taken been,
> Ne had never our lady
> a-been heavene queen.
>
> Blessed be the time
> That apple taken was.
> Therefore we moun singen
> Deo gracias.

According to the fifth-century theologian Augustine of Hippo, Adam's sin has been transmitted from every parent to every child ever since as the result of 'sinful sexual excitement which accompanies procreation'. However, it should be remembered that before his conversion, Augustine had lived with his mistress, fathered a son, and had had plenty of opportunities to identify this 'sinful sexual excitement'. It is ironic that from a man who, enjoying a satisfying sexual life, had prayed to be made holy 'but not yet' and who subsequently treated his former partner and child in a less than Christian way, should come such an argument which has influenced the church in so negative a way.

However interpreted, the story of the first disobedience, the history of the doctrine of original sin and the role played by Eve, has provided problems for women in the past. But from her perspective as a woman, a nun and a theologian, Lavinia Byrne argues that it still poses problems, not only for Christian women but for the whole church today:

> It gives me a problem because the church in general and my church, the Roman Catholic church, in particular uses it as a theological underpinning for a theology which says woman is inferior to man. Woman is created for man in the sense that men are the thinking head of the church and women are the feeling heart of the church.

This has been exacerbated by the fact that Christians understand the principal role of Jesus to have been to reverse the sinful process originated by Adam:

> *For as by a man came death, by man has come also the resurrection of the dead. For as in Adam all die, so also in Christ shall all be made alive.* (1 Cor. 15:21–2)

While the church found the feminine role to be one of seduction and uncleanness and the very source of humanity's misery, the Saviour of the human condition was, in due season, born as a man, Jesus. The theologians and apologists were less happy, however, to acknowledge that had there not been such a sin, there could never have been so great a redeemer. '*O felix culpa, quae talem ac tantum meruit habere Redemptorem*' (O happy fault, which deserved to have so great a Redeemer of such a kind).

Lavinia Byrne argues that the image of woman as inferior to man has been reinforced by the language of Christianity down the ages. The Apostles' Creed, which is the most commonly recited Christian statement of belief, begins with the affirmation, 'I believe in God *the Father* almighty, Creator of heaven and earth'. But the creeds, says feminist theologian Elizabeth Stewart, are only one example of building up a picture of God as male:

> Sally MacFague, a radical feminist theologian, once said if God is male, then male is god. What she meant was that if you use exclusively male imagery of God then the necessary implication is that men are closer to God, that men image God in a fullness that women do not. And this is certainly what Christianity has believed and practised. She has explored the way in which traditional images of God as king, father, all-powerful, all-knowing, perfect, static, transcendent not only reflect the power and experience of the male, they also serve to legitimize the hierarchical patriarchal structures of the church. We have seen that this is the way women have been treated by the church and in countries which have been influenced by Christian theology. They have been regarded as being less than fully human, as being further away from God in some way, and this is why of course there have been the massive battles this century in most of the Christian churches over the ordination of women. It has raised the question of whether women can participate in godly things; whether they can represent Christ the Son of God at the Eucharistic table. And I think all this comes down to the way in which Christianity has tended to use male, and exclusively male images of God.

Through her writing and speaking, Elizabeth Stewart is campaigning for Christians to drop such exclusively male images of God in their language and instead use inclusive language which sees God as neither male nor female. Such a shift would, she believes, help point us back to that equality between the sexes which is found in the original creation story.

Vivienne Faull, formerly Chaplain of Clare College, Cambridge and now Dean of Leicester Cathedral, is a priest who is aware of how the language of liturgy and worship, is also heavily male oriented. She argues that while by baptism all people become full members of the Body of Christ, the language of theology and liturgy often seems to deny their basic equality:

> Women have become increasingly aware of, and vocal about, their exclusion. A language in which a masculine noun or pronoun can be used to denote membership of both sexes reflects a culture where the male is normative. Language which includes only male metaphors for God reflects a culture for which the most sacred is male. As liturgical reformation sweeps through the churches, liturgical revisers in Canada, the United States of America, New Zealand, Australia and England agree that alternatives should be found for such terms as 'men', 'brothers', 'sons', 'mankind'.

But to suggest that a change of heart within religious hierarchies could be achieved simply by attention to syntax and pronouns would be to underestimate the importance of the issue and to confuse the need for clear and radical thinking in the on-going debate on theology and sexuality.

> Drawing on neglected scriptural and spiritual traditions and the reflections of contemporary women, worship and theological understanding is increasingly benefiting from women's experience and insight. With an awareness of inclusive language, the worship of the people of God can begin to include the experiences of all the people of God and the equality given in baptism can begin to influence the structures as well as theology of Christian organizations.

But for some Christians, equality between the sexes can never be achieved while belief in the Christian doctrine of original sin remains current. As we have seen, that has its roots in the story of Genesis when Eve the woman tempts Adam the man to eat fruit from the forbidden tree in the garden of Eden. The fruit eaten, paradise is lost, sin is introduced into the world and our relationship with God and with creation is impaired. God stands in judgement:

The Lord God said to the serpent, 'Because you have done this, cursed are you above all cattle, and above all wild animals; upon your belly you shall go,... all the days of your life. I will put enmity between you and the woman, and between your seed and her seed; he shall bruise your head, and you shall bruise his heel.' To the woman he said, 'I will greatly multiply your pain in childbearing; in pain you shall bring forth children, yet your desire shall be for your husband, and he shall rule over you.' And to Adam he said, 'Because you have listened to the voice of your wife, and have eaten of the tree of which I commanded you, "You shall not eat of it", cursed is the ground because of you; in toil you shall eat of it all the days of your life; thorns and thistles it shall bring forth to you; and you shall eat the plants of the field. In the sweat of your face you shall eat bread till you return to the ground, for out of it you were taken; you are dust, and to dust you shall return.' (Gen. 3:14–19)

For John Polkinghorne there is no question that the story of the creation of Adam and Eve is a literal story of the divine craftsman forming the first human beings. Far more is it an attempt to identify the dawning of self-consciousness in an evolving human race:

I don't think the creation of Adam and Eve is the literal story of the divine craftsman forming the first two human beings. It's difficult to imagine how human beings came to be. I am sure we have a continuous relationship with our hominid predecessors but at some time along that evolving line came the dawning of self-consciousness, perhaps the most remarkable thing that has happened in the history of the whole universe: that conscious beings appeared, that the universe became aware of itself. That is remarkable, a surprising development, and how it happened – how gradually and so on – is beyond our powers either to know or to imagine. The story of Adam and Eve is not a scientific substitute story but a story about the human condition and about the human need for God rather than precisely about how human beings came to be.

I see the Adam and Eve story conveying the truth that human beings cannot live without God. That's the fundamental temptation, the fundamental theory that has gone wrong with life: to believe we are independent, can live without God and can do things our way.

In the story, the serpent whispers in Eve's ear, 'Eat this apple you and you'll be like God, you won't need God any more!' That is a mistake. Human beings need God's grace and God's sustaining power; that is the origin of what has gone wrong with human life. I think that behind the story lies the idea of choosing to be ourselves, and not to accept being God's creatures brought disaster and in some senses death into the world.

It didn't bring literal death. That had been there for millions of years already. Sixty-five million years before, the dinosaurs were killed off and that gave the funny little fuzzy mammals who were our predecessors the chance to grow and take over the evolutionary niche.

What came into the world with the dawning of self-consciousness was mortality, the bitterness of death. When people became self-conscious they realized that they were going to die. They also turned away from God and into themselves and lost contact with the only hope of a destiny beyond death. So death became transience, bitter mortality. That is what I think lies behind that story.

While the stories of creation found in the book of Genesis are of course shared by the Jewish and Christian faiths, Jews have a radically different reading of the text, as Professor John Bowker, the former Dean of Trinity College, Cambridge, and now Fellow of Gresham College, London, points out:

> The stories in Genesis belong first to the Jews. In their reading of the book of Genesis there is no original sin, there is a circumstance in which relationships are in harmony and from which Adam and Eve move on to a new opportunity of living. They may do this through fault but the fact remains that what the Christians call the Fall is in Jewish understanding a fall upwards; it is a fall into new opportunities of being human.
>
> Original sin comes in not in the New Testament but much later in the history of the Christian church. It comes in because the New Testament, and especially Paul, looked at that brilliant, wonderful,

imaginative story of Adam and Eve and saw that after Adam and Eve moved into this new opportunity, relationships began to break up: husbands and wives, parents and children, town dwellers and country dwellers, until you get to the tower of Babel and we are broken up between nations and cities.

It is Paul who especially sees Jesus as the figure who begins to put us together again. We are reconciled to each other and to God. The walls of hostility and division are broken down between Jew and Gentile, between man and woman, between slave and free; the walls of traditional division are broken down. Therefore Paul is saying that Jesus could be thought of as the second Adam who comes to undo what was wrong about that first move into new opportunity. Only later is the 'how' questioned: how does Jesus do this reconciling work? Then there comes about the proposition: maybe there was a kind of fault transmitted from Adam through all generations which is an ab-original fault which has to be dealt with and has been dealt with by Jesus. But that concept is not in the book of Genesis as we read it in the Bible, it is only in the way some people choose to read the book of Genesis.

However, Christians throughout the ages have read the story of the fall of humankind in the book of Genesis as a way of explaining human evil – introduced into the world by original sin. Because the first human beings disobeyed the command of God that they should not eat from the fruit of the tree of life, sin entered the world. In his letter to the church in Rome – part of the collection in the New Testament – St Paul wrote that 'as sin came into the world through one man and death through sin, [and] so death spread to all men because all men sinned' (Rom. 5:12).

John Polkinghorne would see original sin as something so radically human that it is tied in with the evolving self-consciousness of the human race. It is all to do with the human response to growing independence and apparent autonomy:

Original sin is exactly this human desire to go it alone, to do it our way and refuse to acknowledge our status as creatures. Something clearly has gone wrong in human life. There's a sort of twistedness, a way which a country's liberator becomes its next tyrant, how the innocence of youth is replaced by the dusty compromises of middle age. Something has gone wrong with human life, and the diagnosis that is presented to us in the story form [of Gen. 3] is that what has happened is our refusal to recognize our dependence upon God.

But it was Paul's theology that was taken up by early Christian writers and led to St Augustine arguing that as Adam's sin of disobedience has been transmitted from parent to child the whole of humanity has become a 'lump of sin'. This is why, in many traditions, babies are baptized as soon after their birth as possible, and the traditional baptismal ceremony contains elements of exorcism renouncing the devil and all his works.

In the second chapter of the Acts of the Apostles, Peter instructs new converts to 'Repent, and be baptized every one of you in the name of Jesus Christ for the forgiveness of your sins.' But theology did not stand still in the fifth century, and original sin was discussed by theologians of both western and eastern churches. For Thomas Aquinas, original sin was the loss of the supernatural gifts Adam had possessed before the Fall, leaving humanity to the natural operation of their wills and desires. Although contemporary Catholic theology identifies original sin as the loss of sanctifying grace and states that concupiscence is its result and not its cause, Protestants, influenced by the developments in natural science, have emphasized original sin as the human inability to rescue itself from its own fallen state by its own strength or resources.

For Martin Palmer, a Christian environmentalist, the traditional teaching about original sin is like a theological strait-jacket restraining spiritual growth.

For me the rejection of original sin is the rejection of a very mechanistic view of why we are as we are, and also it is the rejection of the way original sin has been used as a sledgehammer to instil into us a sense of profound guilt at just being born. This appalling notion that every child who is born is steeped in original sin which has meant in certain Christian traditions that the very act of sexuality, of procreation, is considered itself to be some awful diseased activity that imputes original sin. I think that has done us much damage.

Keith Ward of Oxford University would argue that this traditional idea of original sin no longer goes unquestioned by modern Christian theologians. After all, as he points out, every baby that is born inherits genetic traits, and is born into social, economic and historical circumstances which are not self-chosen but which dictate future behavioural patterns in character and action that are inevitably disordered:

> Many of us feel unhappy with that traditional idea of original sin because people so often confuse it with the idea that sex is dirty and unclean, or that little babies will go to hell if they are not baptized.
>
> These things I do not believe!
>
> A lot of Christian theologians would say that the idea of original sin is the idea that greed and hatred dominate human life. We are born into a scene where these are the values which are made to seem so attractive and thus it makes it very difficult for us to live lives of moral virtue and to know God. So theologians would nowadays argue that original sin is more a condition than a fault.

If Christians, then, need to rethink the doctrine of original sin they also need to rethink how their faith shapes their view of the environment they share with the rest of the world. In the story of creation, and throughout the Jewish scriptures, everything that God has created, whether that be the components of the earth, animals on the earth, location, or even weather, is a creature of God, utterly dependent upon God. Everything has its place in the wisdom of God, and humanity is part of this order, set on earth to tend and preserve it. The birds and animals were, before the creation of woman, man's friends. Keith Ward again:

> There have been some people in recent years who have argued that the creation stories themselves are responsible for human misuse of the environment because the story does say that humans have dominion over the earth. But of course a Christian view would be that this dominion is only exercised under God. You can't do just as

you like. God created the world as well as the people in the world and so dominion is more like stewardship or care than doing whatever we want.

Environmentalist Martin Palmer would call Christians to go one step further than just 'stewardship' in their care of the environment. He argues that humans have a moral obligation towards non-human creatures because Christians believe in a God who declared the whole of creation to be good: 'and God saw everything that he had made, and behold, it was very good' (Gen. 1:31). After the flood which had inundated the world, God made with Noah, who with his family and the selected animals and birds was the sole survivor, a covenant which was for all creatures. 'And God said, "This is the sign of the covenant which I make between me and you and every living creature that is with you, for all future generations" (Gen. 9:12).

According to St John, it is through Christ that 'all things were made… and without him was not anything made that was made' (John 1:3), and it was for the whole world that Christ offers redemption: 'the creation itself will be set free from its bondage to decay and obtain the glorious liberty of the children of God' (Romans 8:21).

This Christian emphasis on the presence of God in and for the world is, he would argue, inspired by the teachings of the Orthodox church:

> In terms of Christianity, the Orthodox church teaches that we are not here to be masters or stewards, to have a managerial relationship with creation. We are here to have a sacramental relationship, to act as a priest acts before a congregation. Just as a priest takes the bread and the wine – the fruit of the earth and the work of human hands – and through no grace or ability of his own offers this up to God and receives it back, he distributes it to the congregation as a grace, as a blessing. So, the Orthodox church says, our role in creation is to take all that is best and all that is damaged and offer it to God, and then to be a channel of grace, a channel of blessing. Now that is a challenging vision, which is what that writer had twenty-five hundred years ago when he rewrote the story of creation; he said we are not just toys of the gods, but he says our glorious role is simply to be a channel of blessing, and that is something quite revolutionary!

The Roman Catholic church, too, has been concerned for the restoration of ecological balance in the world as a whole. In his letter to priests for Holy Thursday in 1988, Pope John Paul II wrote that 'man has lost the awareness of being the priest for the whole visible world, turning the latter exclusively to himself'.

In her reformulation of the theology of the Holy Spirit, the American theologian Rosemary Radford Reuther, herself a Roman Catholic, has called for a radical rethinking of the Western theological tradition's understanding of the hierarchical chain. She questions the hierarchy of human over non-human nature as a relationship of moral value; she criticizes the right of humans to treat non-human nature as private property and material wealth to be exploited; she challenges the structures of social domination, male over female, owner over worker, that mediate the dominion of non-human nature, and she replaces the understanding of the Spirit as non-material, inferior and dominated with the idea of 'God-ness', but conceives them as the inside and outside of the same thing.

Because religion is practice, it is the practitioners who have formulated creeds, and because religion is a living thing, living practitioners will always devise new interpretations based upon their particular historical and cultural contexts. As we shall see, Christian belief is work in progress and because of this, there will be new formulations, new interpretations and new understandings.

And because practitioners come from every walk of life, and represent every discipline, theological insight and coherence must come, as John Polkinghorne argues, from even those disciplines which might be assumed to be hostile to faith:

> Christians always have to look at the creation story; they have to look at how God is behind the world and what God's purpose for the world is. I think Christians always have to listen to what science says. Christians are trying to follow the God of truth, and while science does not, by any means, provide all the truths it does provide some of it, so Christians should welcome and take on board what science has to say – and that can be very helpful to religion, for example about the insights of evolution.

The evolutionary world is not only a world which is allowed to make itself but it is a world which has a necessary cost to it. If you think of the biochemical processes in cells which enable them to mutate and produce new forms of life – that's the very engine of evolution, the things which have eventually produced you and me; when you think about that you will see that the same biochemical processes will allow other cells to mutate and become malignant. The reason that there is cancer in the world is not that the creator is careless or incompetent, it is the inevitable cost of an evolving world allowed to make itself. That is an insight from science which is a help to religion in its struggle with what is undoubtedly the most difficult problem, which is why there is so much suffering and evil in the world, why the creation which is held to be good never-theless seems to be full of terror as well as beauty. I see that as a help because we are inclined to think that if we had been in charge of creation we would have done it better; we would have kept all the good things like the sunsets and so on, and got rid of all the evil things like diseases and disasters that afflict the world, but the more science understands the processes of the world, the more it sees that things are interconnected. It is in some ways a package deal. You can't have beautiful flowers without having poisonous plants, they all fit together. I think that is a help to religion because it shows that God is not careless in what has been done but the world has certain goods, like the freedom to make itself, but these goods have costs which include disease and disaster.

I think one of the outstanding developments of twentieth-century theology – and it's very widespread in Christian theology – is the recognition that when we say God is almighty, we mean that God can do everything that is in accordance with God's character, but acknowledge that God cannot do things which are against God's character. God can't do evil things. God can't do illogical things – he can't for example make $2+2=5$. The God of love is not a God who can be a cosmic tyrant in tight control of absolutely everything, making everything happen, because the gift of love in creation is the allowing of the other to be itself. Parents know that about their own children. For God, in creating this world, is creating something other than God. God has, in a way, self-limited his power by allowing the other to be and to make itself. Therefore everything which happens in the world is not necessarily in accordance with God's will. I believe that God wills neither the act of a murderer nor the incidence of a cancer, but that God allows both to happen – a world to which he has given a degree of creaturely freedom.

2

Born of the Virgin Mary

A mere fifteen minutes drive from Jerusalem, but culturally a world away in what is called the West Bank, lies Bethlehem. Christian pilgrims from Jerusalem have to pass through a checkpoint, where, at times of major festivals, huge queues of cars back up almost to the outskirts of the city itself. Palestinian pilgrims coming the other way, from the West Bank into the city to pray at the Dome of the Rock, are frequently refused entry, particularly on Fridays – the day of prayer for Muslims – and during the month of Ramadan. The birthplace of Jesus is regarded with suspicion. The successors to the shepherds and inn-keepers are regarded as dangerous and potential trouble-makers by the Israeli Defence Force which guards the checkpoint and the security of Israel.

Long before reaching its narrow streets, one can easily identify Bethlehem by the minarets of the mosques and the crosses on churches which dominate the skyline. Manger Street winds up to Manger Square – Bethlehem's central plaza, until recently a fume-polluted car park – flanked on the west by a police observation post and on the east by the Church of the Nativity, built on the very spot where Christians believe Jesus was born around two thousand years ago.

Not one but three crosses grace the stone exterior, reflecting not only the theological divisions within the church but historic dissensions about the protection of this holy site. Above the centre gable is a Greek Orthodox cross, to the right an Armenian cross and to the left the so-called Jerusalem cross. Like all 'holy places' the Church of the Nativity reflects the history of Christian division and schism. However, in Bethlehem that has some advantage because each tradition celebrates Christmas, the birth of Jesus, on a different date: for the Western church it is 25 December, for the Orthodox it is 6 January and for the Armenian church it is 19 January But on none of these dates can Bethlehem be accurately described as 'the little town', made famous by the nineteenth-century hymn-writer, while 'How still we see thee lie' hardly reflects the atmosphere in modern Bethlehem! Buildings are scarred by bullet holes from the recent Intifada, the square in front of the Church of the Nativity is full of buses and cars pumping out diesel fumes, and economically straitened vendors harass bewildered tourists with trays of pious artefacts.

Originally dedicated on 31 May 339, the original Church of the Nativity was built by the Empress Helena, mother of the Emperor Constantine and an indefatigable pilgrim forever in search of relics. In 529 the original Church of the Nativity was pulled down and replaced by the Emperor Justinian with a church of such splendour, size and beauty that 'none, even in the Holy City, should surpass it'.

This was a period when it was regarded as a pious insurance to mark the sites associated with Jesus' ministry by building splendid places of worship. In the twelfth century Crusaders repaired and developed the building, restoring the ravaged interior decoration and putting on a new roof. With the arrival of the Ottoman Turks early in the sixteenth century, the entrances were modified to protect worshippers from the frequent attacks of their Muslim neighbours and from the looting of marble for their buildings. Now its architectural complexity bears witness to its history of design, destruction and reconstruction, a paradigm of the religious history of the land.

The birthplace itself is in a grotto underneath the main church. Interior design and popular piety have combined to create a candle- and lamp-lit chapel, the focus of which is a fourteen-point bronze star underneath a small altar where pilgrims can read in Latin, *Hic De Virgine Maria Jesus Christus Natus Est:* Here, of the Virgin Mary, Jesus Christ was born.

Different versions of the story of Jesus' birth are to be found in three of the four gospels in the New Testament. A long account with a poetic narrative containing the Annunciation to Mary by an angel – a supernatural messenger – that she was to bear a child, her natural and human reaction of horror at an unwanted and unexpected pregnancy, the subsequent reassurance by the angel and the events leading up to and surrounding the birth of the child is found in the third gospel, that of St Luke (chapters 1 and 2).

The fourth gospel, that of John, contains no simple narrative account of the birth but rather a theological analysis of the genesis of Jesus as 'the one who was to come', the human manifestation of the divine, the incarnate one who in simple terms was to reveal to the human condition not only the potential of divinity but the reality of God, something he could do because from the beginning he had been with God the Father, active in creation and preservation. He is called 'the Word of God':

> *He was in the beginning with God; all things were made through him, and without him was not anything made which was made. In him was life, and the life was the light of men. The light shines in the darkness, and the darkness has not overcome it... And the Word became flesh and dwelt among us, full of grace and truth; we have beheld his glory, glory as of the only Son from the Father... And from his fulness have we all received, grace upon grace. For the law was given through Moses; grace and truth came through Jesus Christ. No one has ever seen God; the only Son, who is in the bosom of the Father, he has made him known.* (John 1:2–5, 14, 16–18)

The account of Jesus' birth as recorded in Matthew's gospel in the New Testament like that in Luke confirms that Mary was a virgin – in other words that Jesus was conceived by Mary without sexual intercourse.

> *Now the birth of Jesus Christ took place in this way. When his mother Mary had been betrothed to Joseph, before they came together she was found to be with child of the Holy Spirit; and her husband Joseph, being a just man and unwilling to put her to shame,*

*resolved to divorce her quietly. But as he considered this, behold, an angel of the Lord appeared to him in a dream, saying, 'Joseph, son of David, do not fear to take Mary your wife, for that which is conceived in her is of the Holy Spirit; she will bear a son, and you shall call his name Jesus, for he will save his people from their sins.' All this took place to fulfil what the Lord had spoken by the prophet: 'Behold, a virgin shall conceive and bear a son and his name shall be called Immanuel (which means, God with us). When Joseph awoke from sleep, he did as the angel ... commande*d. (Matt. 1:18–24)

This is a belief which is affirmed by Christians throughout the world each time they recite the Apostles' Creed, the main profession of faith of the Church: 'we believe in one Lord Jesus Christ who was conceived by the Holy Ghost, born of the Virgin Mary, who became man'.

But according to Bishop Jack Spong, the Episcopal Bishop of Newark, author of *Born of the Virgin Mary*, it is a belief that needs to be seen in its cultural context. Although the Graeco-Roman parallels where children are fathered by gods are remote, their existence does give some strength to a belief in the Christian story.

In the first century virgin births were a dime a dozen. Every time they wanted to describe the birth of someone they thought was larger than life they did so in terms of a virgin birth. Mithra was born of a virgin (or according to Jerome, his birth in primeval times was from a rock, involving no human elements), Plato was born of a virgin (although historically he was the son of Ariston and Perictione, both Athenians of distinguished lineage), Alexander the Great was born of a virgin (although his lineage can be traced to the historical King Philip II and Olympius of Epirus), Romulus and Remus were born of a virgin; so that I'm not impressed with any of that data.

Don Cupitt, an Anglican priest, fellow of Emmanuel College, Cambridge and perhaps one of the most radical of modern theologians, argues that the Virgin birth remains a puzzle:

BORN OF THE VIRGIN MARY 39

It is not easy to say what is meant by the Virgin Birth. Does it mean that Mary gave birth without ever having menstruated? That is medically possible if she conceived in her first cycle. That was one of the possible meanings of the Virgin Birth in antiquity. It could also mean she had never had sexual intercourse or, quite simply, it could mean she was unmarried – a maiden. In Roman Catholic doctrine the Virgin Birth means that Mary remained a virgin even after having given birth to Jesus, but most non-Catholics do not believe that, so there is a variety of explanations of what the phrase means.

But to me it means no more than that Jesus was a full-blooded Jew of the House of David of the tribe of Judah and that is of particular significance. In the gospels he is portrayed as the son of Joseph with brothers and sisters. But the doctrines about Jesus developed, to me anyway, in ways which were at variance with common sense. For example, Jesus' brothers are named twice in the gospels but few Christians when asked can ever name them. That suggests to me that the doctrines of a virgin birth, of the incarnation, have had the effect of concealing the real Jesus and hiding the gospels from us.

Keith Ward says that for any attempt to understand it, the account of the Virgin Birth must be seen in its religious context:

> That Jesus had a miraculous conception is part of that religious context, but it does fit also into a Jewish context, and it relates to the creation story when in creation the Spirit moved over the waters of the great deep of chaos and brought the universe to birth. The story of Jesus' conception by the Holy Spirit actually reflects, repeats in a new way, that story of the Spirit actually bringing to birth a new form of life, in the case of Jesus a human life, which is united in a special way to the life of God.

Other apologists have pointed to the widespread claims of virgin births recorded for other religious innovators: Buddha, Kunti (or Prtha) who in the *Mahabharata* is given a mantra by which she may summon any god she chooses to engender a child upon her, and the claim is made even for Zoroaster himself.

That said, there is little *biblical* evidence for a virgin birth, and it is not even part of the teaching of the early Christian church. Scholars have argued that it was a device to rebut any possible attempt to devalue the ministry of Jesus by charges that he was an illegitimate child or had been conceived out of wedlock. Jack Spong points out that:

The Virgin Birth story does not enter the Christian written tradition until the ninth decade. That means we had a number of Christians before there was ever a tradition of a virgin birth, so it is certainly not essential.

Paul, who does all his writing between, say, 48 CE and 62 or 64 CE, never mentions the Virgin Birth. He has only two references to the origins of Jesus: one is in Galatians where he says *'But when the time had fully come, God sent forth His Son, born of a woman, born under law.'* He is talking about the way every human being is born; there's nothing special about that. He certainly doesn't say Jesus is born of a virgin, he simply says he is born of a woman. He has one other reference to the origin of Jesus in his letter to the Romans where he says *'according to the flesh Jesus is a descendant of the House of David'.* That doesn't sound like a virgin birth tradition.

Then you go to Mark, the first gospel to be written. Mark has no virgin birth story in it whatsoever. Mark has only two references to the family of Jesus. The first is in chapter 3 where, after calling his first followers to work with him, and preaching an early sermon, his mother and brothers come in search of him and ask after him. There Jesus uses the opportunity to tell the congregation that *'whoever does the will of God is my brother, and sister, and mother'.* The other is in chapter 6, where in response to his miraculous healing of a dead girl the amazed crowd ask, *'Where did this man get all this? What mighty works are wrought by his hand? Is not this the carpenter, the son of Mary and brother of James and Joses and Judas and Simon, and are not his sisters here with us?'*

In the Bible the family of Jesus is identified as a mother, at least four brothers who are named and at least two sisters who are not named, and all of them are embarrassed at Jesus. This attitude to Jesus, son and brother, by his family, suggests that they are embarrassed at a man whom they 'think is beside himself' and whom they 'go to take away'. It is very difficult to reconcile these attitudes with the story of the woman who had an angel appear to her and tell her she is going to be a virgin mother and then actually had a virgin birth. You don't get any hint in Mark's gospel that there is any story of a virgin birth tradition that he was aware of.

The first time you get it is in the gospel according to Matthew, which I date from between 80 and 85 CE. And the fascinating thing about Matthew is that he quotes the prophecy of Isaiah chapter 7 verse 14, which we translate as *'behold a virgin shall conceive and bring forth a son',* but Matthew quotes that text from a Greek translation of the Hebrew scriptures; he does not go back to the original Hebrew text. If he had gone back to the Hebrew text of Isaiah, he would have discovered that there is no word for virgin or even a connotation of virgin in that text. The connotation of virgin comes only when you translate the Hebrew world *'alma* with the Greek word *parthenos.* There is a clear connotation of virginity in the Greek word *parthenos* but there is no such connotation in the Hebrew word *'alma.*

By the time you get to the fourth gospel, John, there is no birth narrative. On two occasions John refers to Jesus as the son of Mary and Joseph. Surely John knew of the Virgin Birth tradition. It is the last gospel to be written but he specifically omits it. So the very biblical data in support of this idea of a literalized virgin birth story is very, very shaky.

Professor John Bowker looked at the question of the Virgin Birth from a different, less literal perspective. When asked whether he believed in the doctrine of a virgin conception for Jesus, he accepted that what was intended by the Virgin Birth of Jesus was something significant but not literal.

Do I believe in the Virgin Birth?

Yes I do: at least in the sense that I am affirming very strongly that the initiative came from God in the person of Christ. But I am not prepared to spend, or in my view waste, time in considering some sort of 'under the bedclothes theology'. No one was there, nobody but Mary or perhaps Joseph could possibly know. I understand *why* the stories were written and I prefer not to waste time worrying about whether the male component was supplied by God or not. I am prepared to take the stories for what they are in the Bible: stories told in Hebrew Bible terms about God coming to do for us what we could not possibly do for ourselves.

Professor Bowker may dismiss argument over the Virgin Birth as 'under the bedclothes theology' but the point for Bishop Jack Spong is *why* Mary's virginity has been insisted on by a predominantly *male* Christian church. It is an important question, he says, because of the impact it has had on how women have been viewed in Christianity.

The Christian church traffics in guilt, it seems to me. In dealing with women and defining the issue of women in the Christian faith we came up with the idea that there is only one ideal woman and she is a virgin mother. It is very difficult to be both virgin and mother. You cannot be a virgin mother so it is an oxymoron. So the affirmation that there is only one perfect woman who is a virgin mother makes every other woman feel inadequate and as if there is something wrong with her.

Then the Christian church began to play with that: you are already inadequate, you're never going to live up to that ultimate standard, so you have either got to be a virgin, go to a nunnery and give your life up to the work of the church . . . or else you have got to be a mother. And the church's prohibition on birth control comes out of that mentality because they viewed sex as so evil that its only redeeming purpose was procreation. I think the church has treated women shamefully over the centuries.

That is an analysis with which the former Sister, Lavinia Byrne from the Institute of the Blessed Virgin Mary, would agree. She is convinced that the image of Mary as an untouchable virgin promoted by the Roman Catholic church has been a damaging role model for women:

If you go into a Roman Catholic church, you very often see a statue of the Blessed Virgin Mary where she is wearing a white veil, a blue dress and a sash. She is put before us as someone who is subservient. She is seen holding a prayer book or a lily. But if you think about Mary of Nazareth, the original mother of the Christ child, you see someone who was extremely strong, someone who had the energy once she heard that her baby was going to be born, to race across the mountains and visit her cousin Elizabeth. She is portrayed as being a strong woman. She stays with Jesus through his ministry and is there with him at the cross when he dies.

Now what has the church done with this strong woman? She's been turned into a plaster-cast image. Her power and strength have been dismantled. She has herself in the words of her own Magnificat been cast down. She has not been exalted in a way which says 'here was a strong woman, the first of the apostles, the first of the disciples who proclaimed Jesus and his true identity'. The early church did something quite extraordinary. It proclaimed Mary as being the *theotokos,* the bearer of God, the person who brought the divine child into the world. Subsequently, it seems to me, Christianity has tried to dismantle her, all the way down the line, so we are now being told that she is the Mother of Jesus, the Mother of the Church, the mother of sinful people, the mother of the weak. We're not being told that she is the mother of the strong, of the powerful. We're not being told that she is the sister of those women who are struggling for liberation. But there are countries in the world where she is seen as precisely that, where she is the great friend of the poor and their advocate, and that has a scriptural source. How could any woman listen to the Magnificat without a sense of pride, of challenge?

My soul magnifies the Lord,
and my spirit rejoices in God my Saviour,
for he has regarded the low estate of his handmaiden.
For behold, from henceforth all generations will call me blessed;
for he who is mighty has done great things for me,
and holy is his name.
And his mercy is on those who fear him
from generation to generation.
He has shown strength with his arm,

he has scattered the proud in the imagination of their hearts,
he has put down the mighty from their thrones,
and exalted those of low degree;
he has filled the hungry with good things,
and the rich he has sent empty away.
He has helped his servant Israel,
in remembrance of his mercy,
as he spoke to our fathers,
to Abraham and to his posterity for ever. (Luke 1:46–55)

The Magnificat serves as a privileged point of focus, a fundamental text, among Christian women particularly in the Third World, especially in Latin America where the influence of Mary has always been strong. She is the 'new woman', a servant of God resembling the suffering servant 'who did not count equality with God a thing to be grasped but emptied himself, taking the form of a servant, being born in the likeness of men', expressing the spirituality of liberation. She is seen as a disciple of Jesus, a prophetess through the power of the Spirit whose message condemns relationships of domination and oppression and announces a new order of justice and peace, a new creation even. Mary is a revolutionary who, symbolizing the poor among the children of Israel, will bring about a change of heart. In the base communities Mary is seen less as a queen of heaven, and more as a model and example for the struggling oppressed, because she was a poor carpenter's wife, who gave birth in a stable in great poverty, who had to flee as a refugee to Egypt, and who saw her son tortured and killed.

Another place where Mary is seen as a figure not only of piety but of power is Nazareth, the town where she was born and where, after a period of exile in Egypt, she returned with her family, and where Jesus grew up. Nazareth in his time was an insignificant village in the Galilean hills. Now a town of 60,000 it, no less than Bethlehem, provides pilgrims with a dissonant experience as, among the traffic and stallholders vying for attention, they seek the atmosphere of the Holy House. The vast Church of the Annunciation claims fame as the largest Christian church in the Middle East. In its present form it was consecrated only in 1968, but it stands on the ruins of an earlier foundation dating back to the Crusaders, which in turn had been built upon the fifth-century basilica the Byzantines built over the 'big and splendid cave' in which Mary is reputed to have lived. When he became Prince of Galilee in 1099, the Crusader Tancred's first deed was to build a church in the centre of the city. A Christian presence has been maintained since 1620 when the Franciscans bought back the ruined building and restored it in 1730. It was, during the Easter celebrations of 1999, the scene of confrontation between Christian worshippers leaving the church and local Muslims who, having erected a temporary mosque next door, demanded the right to build a permanent structure on the site.

Nazareth is the home town of Mary and it is the place in Israel where all the feasts associated with Mary are celebrated. On 25 March they celebrate the Annunciation, when the angel appeared to her and told her that she was to have a child, conceived by the Holy Ghost; on 8 December there is the celebration of the Immaculate Conception of Mary, the dogma that, from the moment of her conception, Mary was free from all stain of original sin herself. This is an issue hotly debated from earliest times; it is based on early Christian writings depicting Mary as the new Eve, as her son Jesus was seen as the new Adam.

The most recently acknowledged celebration is the Feast of the Assumption which marks Mary's bodily assumption into heaven. It only became an official Catholic teaching in 1950 when Pope Pius XII declared that when she died Mary was taken up body and soul into heaven. Today in Nazareth the feast day is a public holiday when Christians process around the town carrying an icon of Mary and attending a special mass at the Church of the Annunciation. Nazarenes young and old turn out in their Sunday best to pay homage to the Virgin Mary. When the mass itself is over, everyone gathers in the square outside the church to watch a mock battle enacted between two men brandishing swords, encircled and encouraged by young men chanting their devotion to Mary in a special hymn.

For Bishop Jackinto Boolos Marcuzzo, the Roman Catholic patriarchal vicar in Israel and the Bishop in Nazareth, this presentation is more than devotion to a patron saint:

There is a very popular aspect of the feast, what we call the dance of the swords. The people assemble in the square in front of the church and watch this dance with swords. But what this represents is that the Assumption of Mary marks the victory of good over evil. It is a fulfilment of what we call in the Bible the 'protogospel', which means the promise made to Adam and Eve: a woman would come and defeat evil. And this dance reflects the victory of good over evil, of Our Lady of Nazareth's victory over evil.

The special hymn sung outside the church by the young men of Nazareth is an enthusiastic promise that, for the Virgin Mary, for the Lady of Nazareth, their home town, they would be prepared to give even their blood and their souls.

But the Virgin Mary they celebrate is no alabaster statue or unapproachable virgin, as Bishop Marcuzzo went on to explain. He with his fellow-townsmen is very conscious of the living legacy of Mary and her family to the town today.

When we speak of Our Lady here in the town of Nazareth it is in a special way, and when we talk of her in the Holy Land it is in a more general way. She is not something we learn about from the books. She is not someone we have learned about from a long tradition. She is someone who concerns us as a family. She is like our neighbour. She is someone who is still living with us now and has been at all times. She belongs to my village, to my quarter. When we talk about Our Lady and about Joseph or even about Jesus Christ, for the people of Nazareth we are not speaking of someone who is abstract, but someone who is living. Mary is one of us.

In Nazareth Mary is seen as a friend to turn to in time of trouble and distress – whether political uncertainty, economic hardship or personal heartache. This is also how the Virgin Mary is seen in Bethlehem, the town where she gave birth to Jesus.

Just up the road from the famous and familiar Church of the Nativity and on the right-hand side is another smaller, less well-known, place of pilgrimage. It is the Milk Grotto, a chapel built over a small cavern in the soft white rock. Legend relates that here Mary nursed the newborn Jesus, and a few drops of her milk spilt on to the rock, miraculously turning the surrounding stone white.

Recently restored, the church is cared for by the Franciscans who are the custodians of so many of the Holy Places in the Holy Land. The Milk Grotto houses a collection of paintings depicting Mary breast-feeding the Christ child. Antique Byzantine paintings and Renaissance masterpieces hang side by side with works of popular devotion painted by the faithful from every generation, for whom this aspect of Mary's grace has been specially relevant. It is apparent from many of the paintings, however, that piety has obscured biological function as the infant is portrayed finding nourishment in some singularly unlikely places.

Once a week women from Bethlehem and surrounding villages come to the Milk Grotto to honour the Virgin Mary by attending mass in the place where it is believed that Mary breastfed the child Jesus. It is also to this shrine that Muslim and Christian women bring problems of infertility or illness to a very human Mary – a Mary who knew what it was to be poor and marginalized and burdened with care. It appeals no less to Muslims than Christians because in Islam *Maryam* is the mother of *'Isa,* Jesus. She plays a more prominent role in the Qur'an, where she is mentioned thirty-four times, than in the Bible, where she is mentioned only nineteen. Unlike the Christian development of a theology of Mary, her role in Islam is solely that of the mother of the prophet, who, like all good Muslims, has surrendered herself to the will of God – a clear reflection of Mary's acceptance of her role in the divine economy when she says to the angel of the Annunciation, *'Behold the handmaid of the Lord, be it unto me according to thy will.'*

Her innocence in the face of slanders of sexual impropriety when taking her baby home is supported by no less than a miraculous intervention by her child, who justified her innocence, claiming that he was 'the servant of God'. Throughout Islamic history the purity of Mary has been cherished, and, by later Islam she has been regarded as sinless. Islamic tradition gives us more human details about Mary's parents, her upbringing and her relationship with her child. While many of these may be paralleled in the apocryphal gospels – pious accounts of the life Jesus, his family and ministry which owe more to devotion than any historical fact – it is obvious how they have influenced the popular, and pragmatic, piety of Muslim women. As a result, devotion to the places associated with Mary is no less authentic or genuine for Muslim women than for their Christian sisters. There is an account recorded by the oldest historian of Mecca, Azraqi, that when Muhammad ordered the cleansing of the Ka'aba of its idols and paintings of prophets and angels, he put his hands over a picture of Mary with the infant Jesus on her knee and ordered that while all other paintings be washed over, this alone should be protected.

Brother Lawrence Brodie is the American Franciscan in charge of the Milk Grotto, and he exercises a unique ministry to the pilgrims who regularly visit.

> It is called the Milk Grotto because Mary nursed Jesus here as a baby after she left the Nativity Grotto where the animals were. They needed to take refuge somewhere. They found this cave in order to do that and while feeding the child some drops of milk fell to the ground, turning the grotto white, which is why it is called the Milk Grotto. Both Muslim and Christian woman come here to burn candles. They have special devotions to the Blessed Virgin Mary. Throughout the centuries we have heard of miracles happening where a woman would have a breast cancer and she would come here to take some of the grotto and make it into a powder and drink it. And also for the nourishment of new-born babies; mothers who have just given birth would come here and ask for some of the powder in order to drink it to make their milk more nourishing for their children.

But this is a devotion and faith which is not limited to the past. Regularly women knock at the door of the Milk Grotto and ask the Custodian for some of the white powder. Small plastic phials filled with chalk taken from the grotto are kept for these women. Father Brodie blesses the phial and gives it to the petitioner as a gift. The faith of the petitioner is, he assures, often justified, and many stories of healing, conception and restored marital harmony exist as testimony both to the physical properties of the chalk and the faith of the believers.

For Bishop Marcuzzo in Nazareth this Mary, the Mother of Jesus, is a woman whose virgin birth presents no difficulties:

> The most traditional theology claims that Mary was the Mother of God, the *theotokos,* so we believe that she was the mother of Jesus Christ and she played fully the role of Mother. It is not necessary here to speak of some of the biological aspects of the birth of Jesus or other things which may cast a shadow on the genuine mother-hood of Mary. Without question Mary was really a mother, and all women in the world can consider her a true mother.

And this, too, is how Sister Lavinia Byrne would like to see the Virgin Mary, but it is not, she believes, the way in which Mary has often been presented to Christians by a male-dominated hierarchy:

> A male church very easily teaches a doctrine that makes women afraid of their own sexuality, and I think the Virgin Mary has been brought in as an ally by a male hierarchy to make women feel afraid both of their ability to create and also of their ability to be loving and tender and to be sexual people. The image of a Virgin Mary who is portrayed as chilly, as a white stone statue, has been used to make women afraid of their sexuality. Nowadays we are busy trying to reclaim some of the joy and freedom of that experience of being sexual beings and so we are looking beyond that plastic statue image of Mary to the virgin mother who is somehow more playful and teaches us to enjoy our own autonomy and also enables us to enjoy being sexual beings as well.

Bishop Jack Spong also would argue that it is not only traditional iconography of the Virgin Mary which is anachronistic; the paradigm of subservience is neither creative nor helpful:

> The virgin as she is portrayed is a passive, docile, obedient woman, the kind of woman that every man thinks he wants his wife to be, passive and docile and obedient. But that is not the kind of image which is going to inspire women in the twentieth and twenty-first

centuries. Women have come out of the home place, they've entered the market place, they've entered the world of commerce, they've entered the world of politics, the world of religion. Women are now bishops in the Anglican Communion as well as priests, and the idea that the role of woman is to be a passive, docile, obedient creature is no longer relevant. To have herself ruled by the masculine figure, with her primary role to intercede with the masculine authority – which is primarily the role of the virgin in history – is just not on! I just don't believe that is going to be picked up and celebrated in the Western world.

And indeed it has already been rejected. As early as the 1970s Marina Warner, a well-brought-up, convent-educated, Catholic girl had written *Alone of All Her Sex: The Myth and the Cult of the Virgin Mary* (Weidenfeld and Nicholson, 1976). Drawing on an astonishing variety of sources, art, literature, theology and myth, she argues that for all its power and beauty, the cult of Mary had been, on the whole, a damaging thing. Although as virgin, mother, queen, bride and mourner, Mary has been the symbol of the feminine that continues to direct the imaginations and hearts of men and women, it has been a symbol which has been damaging, above all damaging for women, who, in the church's idealization of Mary, have been denigrated not exalted. Mary, alone, of all her sex had pleased the Lord. The church had been unable to cope with femininity. Woman was Eve, temptress and harlot, and only Mary, pure virgin and perfect mother, had escaped the blight of Eve.

Following the earlier work by Marina Warner, this negative theology is being pragmatically rejected by many women who today are translating their rejection of Catholic tradition into actions as extreme as leaving the Christian church, according to Lavinia Byrne. She believes that they are not rejecting Christianity but rejecting a church which doesn't see them as equal with men.

I know a large number of women in their forties who now say 'I've brought up my children in this church but now frankly it gives me nothing. It doesn't sustain me any longer, it merely tells me I am a sinner and now I am going to go because I am going to find succour elsewhere. I am going to find groups of women who share my feelings.' This is happening all across the world where there are women who get together, who meet in each others' homes and in their gardens to celebrate together Eucharists, liturgies which are not recognized by the church but which are nonetheless thanksgivings which they can offer in total good faith to a God whom they are now seeing not as strictly male and whom they want to worship in spirit and in truth.

Feminist theologians have argued that if the cardinal sin for men is the sin of pride, then for women the cardinal sin is 'hiding', 'failing to speak their own truth', 'allowing themselves to be marginalized and subordinated'. And if empowerment is what women need, then Christianity and the structures of the church cannot provide it, and women would be better off spending their energies on alternative spiritualities.

Bishop Vincent Nichols recognizes that his church's teaching on the Virgin Birth may have alienated some women but, he would argue, it is not the whole picture:

I think it is capable of bearing a different interpretation, and the interpretation I would rather give it is much more of the uniqueness of the event of Christ's conception and birth and what that does to raise our whole perception of the physical reality in which we live our lives and overcome the dualism which is so much one of the hallmarks of pagan life. It is actually an integrating mystery rather than a separating mystery, and somehow it can equally be seen to defend and uplift the dignity of women at a time when, even more than today, they were at the margins of society .

It says that the archetypal way of co-operation with God is somehow seen in the sensitivity and total responsiveness of this woman, and therefore the title I like for Mary the best is that she was the first and most responsive disciple. She embraced the word of God as all Christians are asked to do to such an extent she gave it her flesh. And in that sense it says if you want an icon of discipleship, of what it is to be a Christian, then look at that woman who gave herself to him and co-operated fully and opened up the path of discipleship which is proper for all of us.

Eamon Duffy, Reader in Church History at the University of Cambridge, has argued that the decisive theological moment for the position of Mary was the decision by the Council of Ephesus (431 CE) that she should be given the title *Theotokos:* God-bearer, softened in western usage to *Mater Dei*, Mother of God.

> The title was designed to say something about Christ rather than Mary, to assert and protect the reality of the Incarnation by insisting on the absolute identity of the eternal Word of God with the man Jesus. To call Mary the God-bearer was to assert that in her womb God had once and for all thrown in his lot with humanity, had joined us, holding nothing back. Mary was not a pipe through which the divine spirit inserted itself into earthly matter, or a bag in which the precious spice of the Godhead was temporarily contained, but the intimate source of the human identity of God himself, giving God incarnate all that a mother gives to her children – blood, bone, nerve and personality. In her conceiving and childbearing, heaven and earth were wedded beyond any possibility of divorce; a stupendous miracle had occurred which raised human nature to heaven itself.

Don Cupitt expresses concern that so much attention to the doctrine of the Virgin Birth has distorted the significance of Jesus himself:

> We no longer see Jesus as a human being or as a teacher. Try asking people in the street what Jesus' teaching actually was and you'll get surprisingly vague answers, and in the Christian creeds, Jesus' teaching has disappeared.
>
> He was a prophet of the Kingdom of God, someone who sought to bring about religious insight by dramatic reversal sayings and parabolic stories. Someone who tried to teach a new kind of life, living by the imagination, living in response to what he called God – in the present moment. The best and most vivid interpretation of Jesus' teaching is the Sermon on the Mount. It starts with the Beatitudes and then all the sayings where Jesus revizes and radicalizes traditional Jewish duties like prayer or fasting or

almsgiving. He demands something like an inner transformation of the self so that we shall be completely responsive to experience and no longer egotistic or anxious. He is not a traditional doctrinal teacher, he does not seek to draw attention to himself. He talks about this strange new way of life which he calls the Kingdom of God or eternal life, and he uses language in such a way as to blow our minds and to open our imagination to the possibility of living in a completely different way.

But Dr Duffy argued in his Aquinas Lecture (1998) that the Second Vatican Council drastically re-orientated the basis of Mariology by including what they had to say about Mary within the framework of one of the Council's most significant documents, *Lumen Gentium*. The doctrine of Mary was firmly placed within the doctrine of the Church; she should then be seen in the wider context of the work of Christ and the role of the universal church. But, he goes on to say, while the door had been opened for a rediscovery of the Madonna which does not maim, little post-conciliar teaching has followed this up, concentrating disproportionately on the Annunciation story in St Luke's gospel, and the church has continued to see Mary as essentially a model of obedience to God. In spite of the Council, the Church has preferred the plaster saint!

Yet Mary as a role model for all humanity was behind the most recent campaign to get the Pope to elevate the status of Mary before the beginning of the new millennium. Since 1993, four and a half million Catholics from 157 countries have signed petitions asking the pope to pronounce Mary as *Co-redemptrix, Mediatrix of all graces and Advocate for the people of God*. Each month one hundred thousand more Catholics add their voices to the call for change.

Professor Mark Miravalle, a theologian at the Franciscan University of Stubenville, Ohio, is responsible for the petition. He is keen to point out that Mary's new title would not put her on an equal footing with Christ, as some Catholics have feared: so what would it mean?

The title co-redemptrix is perhaps the most misunderstood, particularly in the English language because the prefix co- often has the connotation of equal. Well, quite to the contrary, co- comes from the Latin word *cum* which means with, as St Paul in scripture calls all Christians to be co-workers with Jesus, to be with Jesus but never to be on the level of equality with Jesus. So too Pope John Paul II on six occasions has used the title *co-redemptrix* for Mary, and that title in no way places Mary on the same level as Jesus Christ but rather honours her unique participation with and under Jesus Christ in the work of Redemption. So therefore when the Catholic church speaks of Mary as *co-redemptrix*, or if you will a mother suffering for her children in the spiritual life, this in no way seeks to raise the position of Mary to the level of divinity but rather to enable Christians to understand that we do have a spiritual mother. In a real sense Mary is the mother of all humanity.

Professor Miravalle discussed this call for Mary's new status several times with the Pope and he was confident that the Pope would respond before the beginning of the new millennium and establish the publicly-enhanced status for the Mother of Jesus. One reason,he suggests, for such a confirmation is that, at the end of a materialistic and destructive century, the Virgin Mary is becoming increasingly important to people throughout the world.

Many people of the human family want a spiritual mother. They want a being who loves them and cares for them in the model of maternity, and this is why the role of Mary has become much more popular, not only within Christian circles but even outside it. Faiths like Islam have a very strong devotion to Mary. We are seeing more and more appreciation of the fact that with the fatherly revelation of God we also have a motherly manifestation in this perfect human being, the mother of Jesus.

That is why Professor Miravalle claims there have been more visions of the Virgin Mary in the last thirty-five years than in the last three centuries. New liturgies have been created and churches world-wide have been dedicated to her. For Lavinia Byrne the time is ripe for women to retrieve the Virgin Mary as a source of great strength in an uncertain world:

I go and light candles to her and every time I do this, I say to her, 'This is a subversive candle which I am lighting.' I am saying to her, 'Please help the church realize that if it builds itself uniquely as a male institution it is doing women a great disservice. It is not just excluding *us,* it is excluding *you!* So to get you back and to get us back on scene we need all of us to work together, women to become more visible, women to become more powerful and women to have more say in the way the church is run and how it operates.'

Lavinia Byrne would argue that Mary is reclaiming women for the church and that in the church women are reclaiming Mary for the rightful representation and validation of their work for the church.

I think the Virgin Mary is turning out to be a very keen supporter of women worldwide. I have noticed what happens when women call upon her and ask for her aid. She gives them a source of strength and energy to go out and say that these structures are not good enough: we must go out and make the world a better place.

For Professor Miravalle, however, the Virgin Mary's message to Christians today is far wider, and goes beyond challenging sexism in the church:

I think Mary has to say at this time in history what she has also said in the early church, that she is a spiritual mother given by Christ from the cross not only to every Christian but to every human being, and that as spiritual mother she seeks spiritual benefit for her children. Her greatest desire is to unite all her children with her first child, Jesus Christ. So I think that the words of Mary today are the same as they were at the wedding in Cana, which was to do whatever he tells you to do, in reference to Jesus, for the spiritual peace and for the spiritual benefit of the human family.

While such charismatic protagonists single-mindedly seek to propel Mary further into the minds and devotions of the faithful and even more confirm her role in the redemptive process, it should not be forgotten that hostility to the elevation of Mary and the development of devotion to her has always been seen as the touchstone of

Protestantism which at the Reformation reacted strongly against Marian devotion, partly owing to its rejection of the cult of saints and partly in keeping with a more positive view of sex and the married state. Once a married priesthood had been endorsed as the norm, vocation to a celibate and virginal state could no longer be held up as an ideal. It was the German Protestant theologian Karl Barth who wrote in his immense and appropriately titled *Dogmatic Theology* 'In the doctrine and worship of Mary there is disclosed one heresy of the Roman Catholic Church which explains all the rest.' It is because Christians are so very varied and reflect such a spectrum of theological positions, all dependent upon the undisputable fact that Mary was the Mother of Jesus whom all Christians confirm to be their saviour and redeemer, that the role of Mary can no longer be ignored by Protestants or unquestioningly monopolized by Catholics. Rita Crowley Turner, a Catholic writer and broadcaster, argues that Mary is a useful catalyst in ecumenical encounter:

> In Mary the Christian recognizes a human person who offers no resistance to the power of God. She co-operates with God, she works with God. The consequence of Mary's personal acceptance of God's grace was to bring the Saviour into the world, where he would free all humankind from sin; she can be considered the channel of grace for all. Some believe that faith alone justifies; others that faith increases as believers struggle to express the action of grace in their lives. In Mary faith and work were one. She is the human perfection of the Spirit. She is the mother of the Saviour and therefore, at least physically, at the centre of Christianity. Mary was the point at which God and the human were united. She as an example of faith and unity can be identified as the hope of all Christians.

And it is as such that she was seen as the inspiration of the Ecumenical Society of the Blessed Virgin Mary, an inter-denominational society founded in England in 1966 'to advance the study of the place of the Blessed Virgin Mary at various levels in the Church under Christ and to promote ecumenical devotion'. Such movements are just one sign of hope that when Christians unite to affirm their belief in Jesus Christ, they can find agreement not only in his conception by the Holy Ghost but in a generous understanding of the role played by the Virgin Mary in the operation.

3

Jesus: True God and True Man

Regardless of its geographical location, in Palestinian territory, Bethlehem could almost be a suburb in Jerusalem's sprawling conurbation. On the left-hand side of the road travellers can see a flat hill-top, the site of one of Herod's palace fortresses and used by the Zealots in the Great Revolt in 70 CE and later in the second century by the soldiers in the Bar Kochba revolt which was finally subdued in 135 CE. On the ridge to the right-hand side lies Tantur, an ecumenical institute. Set up after the Second Vatican Council, it is a curiously located study centre. For Palestinians who fear harassment, refusal, or worse at the checkpoint into Jerusalem, it provides a possible alternative route into the city – possible only at times because when the Israeli authorities are determined to prevent entry to Jerusalem, extra border guards will be patrolling the roads, even the fields, around the Institute, forcing Palestinians back into the West Bank territory.

International diplomatic initiatives have urged that Jerusalem should finally, because of its special character, be designated under international supervision a so-called *corpus separatum*, protected as an area of particular concern. There would be free right of entry for members of all three of the monotheistic religions, ensuring their freedom of worship and appropriate protection in the city. The issue of religion, therefore, becomes even more politicized in Jerusalem's municipal offices. It is the desire of the Jerusalem authorities to claim the 'little town of Bethlehem' as their own. King David, founder of Jerusalem and grandson of the faithful Ruth, was born in Bethlehem, and Rachel, long regarded as the mother of the nation, is buried there. She died giving birth to Benjamin, and her tomb is one of Judaism's most significant centres of devotion for Jewish women worldwide. Like Sarah, Rachel was barren for many years of her marriage to Jacob and her tomb is visited by women praying for children. Significantly it is recorded in Jeremiah that when the Jews passed her tomb on their way to exile in Babylon she wept for them in heaven and prayed for their return. The original tomb was built in the Middle Ages, while the site was identified, expanded and protected as a result of the work of Moses Montefiore, the nineteenth-century philanthropist.

In 1997 the city fathers celebrated the three thousandth anniversary of the establishment of Jerusalem as the capital of King David – a somewhat arbitrary date and a celebration which elicited much critical and even derisory response from Europe and the Arab world. As a result of this, Bethlehem, David's birthplace, received some considerable attention and Rachel's tomb was walled in to 'protect it' from non-Jewish interference.

While the patriarchs Abraham and Sarah, Isaac and Rebecca, Jacob and Leah are all buried in Hebron, Rachel, Jacob's second wife, who died in childbirth, is buried on the outskirts of Bethlehem. Much as the Milk Grotto is a focus of pilgrimage and devotion for Christian and Muslim women, so the tomb of Rachel is a focus of devotion and hope for Jewish women who go there to pray for fecundity. In the middle of the building lies the huge tomb, a velvet-draped, monolithic cenotaph, with a scarlet thread wound around it seven times. Small pieces are snipped off and given to pilgrims as talismans to aid conception, for a safe childbirth, for the wellbeing of sickly infants, or to ward off sickness. There is even a website and a global federation of women called Rachel who are invited to share Rachel's role as 'mother of the nation', to pray regularly and give material support for the upkeep of the site.

But notwithstanding the Jerusalem city authority's attempts at claiming Bethlehem primarily as a Jewish centre of pilgrimage, for

Christians Bethlehem will always be the place where Jesus was born. It is the 'little town' of the Christmas carol where 'the wondrous gift is given' and 'where God imparts to human hearts the blessing of his heaven'.

Despite the recent *intifada* which has left many of Bethlehem's buildings bullet-marked, and entry to its Holy Places guarded by watchful soldiery, it will always be the place which Christians, wherever they are, and however they understand or interpret the Incarnation, identify as the place where at one moment in history, God came down to earth: the divine was made human and sense could be made of all that had gone before. It was the event which put the wanderings of the patriarchs into context, which justified domestic division, national upheavals and exiles and enabled the typologies of the Jewish experience to be understood.

In spite of political dislocation, *intifada* and resultant tensions, Christians from all over the world have gathered at the Church of the Nativity on Manger Square each year to celebrate the birth of Jesus some two thousand years ago.

Regardless of the season, pilgrims throng the church and almost shyly duck through the doorway at the head of the stairs which leads to the crypt, the site of the original stable or cave where it is believed Jesus was born. Throughout the year, groups of pilgrims gather to sing carols in a dozen languages; brief liturgies are led by Christian leaders of a hundred denominations. Some of the faithful stand, others kneel, but most, regardless of religious tradition, genuflect to kiss the silver star set into the floor at the place where, so tradition has it, the manger stood.

Even if it were not the right place, even if tradition had got it wrong, the faith and devotion of generations of pilgrims have made this place special. The holiness is of place, of tradition and of practice: stones have been made holy by the prayers of the faithful.

There can be no small irony that this place, now the centre of world-Christendom's devotion, was once the outhouse of a first-century inn, the place where donkeys were kept and a site chosen simply because there was no room inside the inn. As in Nazareth, many houses in Bethlehem incorporate some of the many caves that honeycomb the hillsides. The cave provides a natural apse to the house, a safe place of protection for animals. No mention is made in the gospels of a cave, but from the second century Christian writing has referred to the *cave* where Jesus was born. Even today the hillside caves are used for stabling and protecting animals.

The Greek Orthodox Archbishop Theophilus, combining information with a pastoral concern for the pilgrims he greets, makes an impressive guide to the grotto of the Nativity:

> Here is the actual place of the birth of Our Lord and Saviour Jesus Christ, and here this star is a symbolic star which marks the actual place. Above it is an altar where every day the divine liturgy is conducted. So I witness each day people from all nations, Christians and people from other religions as well, and it is true that no-one who approaches Christ ever goes away without gaining something.

For the Palestinian Christians born and living in Bethlehem, familiarity does not breed contempt. There is a real sense of continuity: there are still sheep on the hills outside the town and although the shepherds often wear flak jackets and carry rifles, there is a real sense that it was their immediate predecessors who *'came with haste to the place where the young child lay'*.

Just up the road from Manger Square and the Church of the Nativity in Bethlehem is the Evangelical Lutheran Christmas Church. To be the pastor of such a place has a particular poignancy for the Bethlehem-born Mitri Raheeb:

> For me Bethlehem as a city is a very important place because it is a reminder that our faith is not a myth but it is something that took place in history, in a certain place at a certain time in a certain context. And Bethlehem is a reminder of that fact. The name Bethlehem means the *city of bread* in Aramaic, and for Christians Bethlehem is the city of bread in the sense that Jesus is the Bread of Life which, through his coming, means that he shares his life with us.

Christians believe Jesus was the Son of God who was also born a human being – in other words that he was both human and divine. This doctrine of the Incarnation, as it is called, is at the heart of Christian understanding about the person of Jesus Christ. Mitri Raheeb explained that:

> In the Greek language the word for incarnation means that God has pitched a tent in the midst of the human beings who have their tents pitched all around him and he became one of us and lived among us. I think this is a very powerful picture and a very powerful message of Christianity: Christ sharing his life with us, sharing our suffering but not sharing our sin. One of the Eastern Fathers from Egypt once said that God became human so that we humans might become the image of God.

For Palestinian Christians, the image of a tent being pitched in their midst is particularly poignant. Many have lost their homes and their land and are refugees in their ancestral homelands, and many find the parallels between the holy family's exile in Egypt and their own dislocated lives singularly relevant. Much as contemporary theological debate has restored the Jewish elements to the Christian understanding of the life and ministry of Jesus, so contemporary Palestinian theologians seek to restore the element of nationhood to him. His presence in their wanderings, homelessness and uncertainty is the essence of incarnation.

Canon Naim Ateek, formerly responsible for the Arabic-speaking congregation at St George's Cathedral in Jerusalem, is the founder of the Sabeel Liberation Theology Centre, an organization committed to ecumenism and to issues of peace and justice.

> A theological outlook on Christ is very real to people here: whether they understand it enough to explain it is something else, but it is deeply embedded in people's minds. To see Christ in a theological way enables those of us working with Palestinian Liberation Theology to understand Jesus Christ and emphasize him as the model for faith as a human being. He was the Palestinian Christ who lived under occupation and who formulated his teaching and

ministry within that context and so becomes an example of that faith. He is a person who can inspire us in how we should behave under occupation, how we should respond to people in power, whether religious or political leaders. So while, at one level, there is the human Jesus who is our brother in the conflict, in the suffering of the Palestinians, our companion through life today in Palestine, there is also the Lord of history, the Saviour, the person who liberated us. There is Jesus as the liberator who died and rose again.

That doctrine of the Incarnation is equally central for Western Christians in their understanding of Jesus Christ. Professor John Bowker is the former Dean of Trinity College, Cambridge, now Fellow of Gresham College, London:

The whole of Christianity comes from three words in Greek in the Gospel of Mark, chapter 6 verse 2. The people look at all that Jesus is saying and doing and ask the simple question – three words, *pothen tauta touto* – From whence these things to this man? Or as the Revised Standard Version of the Bible has it, *Where did this man get all this?* All of Christianity is the answer to that question, and Jesus himself gave parts of the answer to that question because he said, *'All that you see me doing, all that you hear me saying is not coming from myself, I couldn't do all this. It is coming from God and it is being mediated through my person.'* So Christians have to say that he was totally human – there can be no compromise – and yet, at the same time, God was wholly, consistently and unequivocally present in that humanity in such a way that people were driven to ask the question, where is he getting all this power from? The answer of Jesus to this question is that it is coming from God whom he can speak of as other than himself but yet who is wholly present in and through himself.

And it is that dynamic between Jesus the human being and Jesus the divine son of God that excites the British feminist theologian Elizabeth Stuart:

Jesus to me is a very revolutionary figure, a very alive figure because he comes across as a very human figure, and I think that is what makes Jesus so exciting to me. As a Christian I believe in some sense this person was and is God and yet this person is also so obviously human. To give an example. The Syrophoenecian woman is an outsider, a Gentile, but who, nevertheless, comes to Jesus and asks him, 'Heal my daughter'. Jesus says, 'No, I won't. I am called only to the lost sheep of Israel' and she argues with him and changes his mind. I find that terribly exciting. Here is someone who is in some sense God but is prepared to be engaged by humanity and in some senses to be changed by humanity. That humanity and God are in that kind of close intimate relationship where they can change each other.

Jesus lived and worked among the people of first-century Palestine. That sense of his life being rooted in a certain time and place is an important aspect of the Incarnation for those who live in the Holy Land today. Bishop Riah Abu Elassel is a Nazarene who lived and worked in Nazareth as the Anglican vicar before he became co-adjutor Bishop of Jerusalem.

We believe that Jesus Christ was a member of the Nazarene community who spent most of his life in Nazareth, and the story of his presence in our midst has been carried on from one generation to another. People could take you and show you places where he lived, where he worked with his mother. For us the historical aspect of the life of Jesus is as important as the aspect of the Word becoming flesh and dwelling among us.

Jesus dwelt among the Jews of Palestine – in the Galilee and then in Jerusalem. He was of course himself a Jew. Christianity only began after his lifetime. And it is the Jewish Jesus whom Linda Brayer, a South African Jew who became a Catholic in Israel in the 1980s, recognizes:

The way he talks when they speak about him – 'he talked with authority' – I know what he means. Judaism has this concept of authority. He comes along and he says, 'Hey wait a minute, you're all into ritual cult taboos, into taboos surrounding purification. You're all into yourself. That's not what it is about.' Jesus opens our minds and our hearts into what is ultimately developed in Christianity – relationship. He deals with the most problematic parts of Judaism, the relationship between Jews and non-Jews. As a Jew who became a Catholic that is what touches my heart, because having been a Jew I have gone from the tribe into the cosmos. I've gone from small closed-in tribe into the world of one human family. And I think that Jesus has shown this to us by his healing of the non-Jews. Jesus himself sets up relationships with non-Jews, Jesus himself approaches Judaism and says we have to do things, to serve our Lord in ways which enhance human life and not just Jewish life. Now Paul picks this up when he says there is no difference between Jew and Gentile. Paul didn't make that up. That's one of the central messages of Jesus. And because he was Jewish and I was Jewish, I know where he is coming from!

With the Shoah (the Hebrew word for catastrophe and the term preferred by Jewish writers to describe the Holocaust), Christian relations with Jewish people were transformed. The Council of Christians and Jews, formed during the Second World War, has nobly struggled against forms of anti-semitism, or anti-Judaism as the late Charlotte Klein argues in her book *Christianity and Antijudaism*. Whereas the term anti-semitism was coined late in the nineteenth century by a journalist, Wilhelm Marr, anti-Judaism had been the currency of Christian theologians who – failing to recognize their role in the redemptive pattern – viewed the Jews as the killers of Christ.

Christian theologians have been forced to re-think the historical assumptions on which traditional theology has been based. Much serious scholarship about Jesus had been anti-semitic. Much interpretation of Judaism at the time of Jesus has been inaccurate. The assumption that post-exilic Judaism had betrayed the prophetic faith of Israel, even to damaging God's covenant with his people, was distorted. Christian liturgists have been forced to re-think their use and interpretation of the traditional lectionary readings for Holy Week. Ancient prayers which have relegated the Jewish people along with 'Turks and infidels' as beyond redemption have had to be re-written. Finally they have been forced to recognize that without the

Judaism of the first century with its distinctive schools, there could have been no Jesus and no Christianity. With the realization that Jesus was born and lived as a Jew, and indeed as we shall see later, was killed because he was a Jew, Christianity's understanding of itself, its history and the tradition from which it was born, has undergone a radical re-evaluation.

Canon Naim Ateek also recognizes this Jewishness of Jesus:

> I can understand why many scholars after the Second World War started emphasizing the Jewishness of Jesus and I think that was a very important development, because many Western Christians were persecuting Jews almost in the name of Jesus himself, and many had forgotten the roots of their faith, forgotten who Jesus was and what his background was. They had forgotten that he came out of a Jewish mother, from a Jewish family, and so when scholars started emphasizing the Jewish nature of Jesus, it sent an important message to Western Christians that they must remember that they cannot persecute Jews. When they thought of Jesus as a Jew, saw him in his Jewish context, it was hoped they would be much more sympathetic to the Jews. I believe that it was a very important development because of the sin of anti-semitism and the sin of the Holocaust.

Naim Ateek suggests that such an imbalance in understanding the person of Jesus and such a distortion of his real message and person has to some extent been rectified, and as scholars have rediscovered the Jewishness of Jesus, of the milieu into which he was born and against which he lived his life, a more authentic picture has been revealed. His was a Jewish life whose practice was dictated by the presence of the Second Temple in Jerusalem with all the sacrificial and purificational rites, the different schools of scholars, priests and rabbis who taught and interpreted the scriptures in different ways, and the petty jealousies inherent in any religious bureaucracy. It is this development which, he argues, has enabled a generation of scholars and believers to understand Jesus' actions as those of an observant Jew and recognize the revolutionary nature of much of what he preached and what he did. He was also an observant Jew living under the yoke of Roman slavery in a province where even the office of Chief Priest was an appointment subject to political forces.

> Now I believe Western Christians need to move on. They need to see Jesus as a Palestinian, because Palestinians are identified by many Western Christians only as terrorists. They have stereotyped the Palestinians in a very negative way. I believe we need to help Western Christians identify Jesus as a Palestinian because he lived in Palestine, he came out of Palestine. Hopefully when people see Jesus as a Palestinian, they will begin to be much more compassionate to the Palestinians and their need for peace and justice, just as Jesus himself felt the need for justice and peace in his own day for his own people. I feel it is right to begin to see Jesus as the Jesus of Palestine in order to bring justice, reconciliation and peace to this part of the world.

Canon Naim Ateek works for peace, justice and reconciliation through Sabeel, a Christian Palestinian Liberation theology centre he founded in Jerusalem. He says the work of the centre is inspired by the person of Jesus – the Jesus who lived under Roman occupation in the first century.

> Sabeel is an Arabic word with a double meaning: it means a path and it also means a spring of water. The name itself reflects the way Sabeel sees its ministry because we are walking on the road of life. It reminds us of Jesus who was the way, the truth and the life, and also the living water. So our ministry has two main objectives. We like to think of ourselves as advocates for Christian Unity so we de-emphasize denominationalism and we try to bring Christians together, regardless of their denominational background, trying to help them to love each other more and help them to see themselves as Christians trying to be faithful to Christ and serving today in their different communities.
>
> The other major emphasis has to do with a prophetic message; the importance of justice as the basis of peace, as the basis of reconciliation, trying to sound a prophetic voice in the midst of the oppression and injustice that we feel. We have a number of programmes that promote these things, working with local clergy,

young people and adults to promote the Christian Unity aspect. At a political level we have a newsletter, different programmes, we speak to groups who come from outside to help them understand who the Christians of the Middle East are, and who the Palestinian people are, and we try to help them understand the complexity of the political situation and how they can be peacemakers with us today.

Palestinians today, Naim Ateek believes, identify that with their own situation since the creation of the State of Israel in 1948.

Jesus is a role model for us because he was able to cope with living under occupation and still emerge as a full human being. He was a person who was really able to deal with injustice and difficulties and still maintain an inner peace and inner freedom, and relate to people as a free person. That is something we need when so many of us feel depressed because we are living under an oppressive regime. Jesus had that quality of life but his relationship with the Father was such that he was able to live life abundantly and to its fullest in spite of the difficulties and injustice around him. That's why we see Jesus as the inspiration for our lives, because he has passed this way before us, he has experienced what we now experience. So when we hear Jesus saying to his followers, 'Love your enemies', he is saying it within the context of living under occupation. When Jesus saw that his ministry had to do with proclaiming liberty and justice, it is really exactly the same thing that we are trying to do now: imitating Christ and trying to learn from him how to live our life today, allowing his power to work through us because we believe he has walked this road before us.

I see Jesus as a rebel because he rebelled at everything unjust. This was the Jesus who had compassion on the crowds, the poor, the oppressed, but at the same time there he was, this person who could identify the corruption within the religious establishment – and he did not fear to stand and confront the religious leaders. He also had the courage, even when he was being condemned, to confront the political leaders and address them and lift before them the truth.

We see Jesus the revolutionary but a revolutionary who was working to bring God's Kingdom on earth, to fulfil the purposes of God for all people, and most of his ministry was done on the periphery because it was there where he felt he could relate to people and carry on a ministry that has that radical element. He was steering religion away from the way humans had almost imprisoned it. It was as if God was being imprisoned within human-made laws and regulations, and Jesus was shattering that, trying to give us a new life, creating a relationship between God and humans as a way of introducing the Kingdom of God for all people. So although we see Jesus as the revolutionary, we see Him as a revolutionary who was working to bring God's Kingdom on earth.

But this interpretation of Jesus as a revolutionary role-model is just one of the more recent interpretations. Theology and practice have encouraged Christians to understand and reinterpret Jesus in their own situations, and nowhere has this been more effective than in Latin America. A recently published poster portraying Jesus in a style more easily identifiable with the famous black and white poster of Che Guevara as a freedom fighter has stirred up controversy in the English countryside, but it is only the most recent interpretation of Jesus the militant. While for most Christian congregations in Britain the army fatigues may reflect current fashion trends, for Christian congregations facing political, military and even clerical persecution, the militant Christ has been a serious inspiration to action and valour. The concept of *Christus Victor*, of Christ as victor, was historically understood as reflecting the Christian conviction that Jesus Christ overcame all the powers of evil and the devil and, while underlying the major theories of the atonement, with its reinterpretation it has inspired the spread of Liberation Theology.

Perhaps *Theologies* of Liberation would more accurately describe the many contemporary movements which seek to explore and discover, express and reflect the presence and power of God in the lives and struggles of oppressed peoples. For many living in the poverty of South American *favelas*, or in parts of Africa or Asia, life as it is experienced must be hard to reconcile with the concept of the redemptive purpose of God as manifested in the role of Jesus and taught by traditional theology.

Liberation theologies aim to combine a faithfulness to God's promise of a fullness of life which embraces economic, political, cultural and spiritual elements with the often contradictory realities of a particular geographical or political context. While Liberation Theology has been particularly associated with conditions in Latin America, there are similar movements in other geographical regions. *Minjung* theology is an indigenous theology deeply-rooted in the culture and religions of the Korean people. *Coconut* theology grows out of the Pacific experience. *Black* theology, a term originally used to describe the theology resulting from the American slave experience, but more recently applied to the experience of the apartheid system in South Africa, chooses for its departure point social relations, particularly the cry of the oppressed. The black experience has been synonymous with poverty, ignorance, terror, exploitation and relegation. *Feminist* theology takes seriously the criticism and conclusions of modern feminism and as well as broadening understanding of inclusive language seeks to review history from a different perspective.

They are all practical responses to the life of Jesus. The first theology of liberation took root in Central and South America in the 1960s. It questioned the authority and tradition long unquestioned in the Roman Catholic Church. It questioned established church hierarchies, and argued that, with its history of repression, of clerical identity with the powerful, the church was beyond reformation and must be replaced by a church arising from the people, themselves inspired by the power of the Holy Spirit. It must literally be a popular church.

While Christianity has usually considered any renewal by the Holy Spirit to be a personal experience, a private matter, within South America it is often a communal experience, an enabling, which results in groups of people working together simply to survive; it is the very renewal of the church. This has often led to the establishment of base communities made up of small groups of ordinary Christians.

Margaret Hebblethwaite is a Catholic writer who has visited and studied many such base communities from El Salvador to Nicaragua.

Following the traditional marks by which Christians identify the church, 'that she is One, she is Holy, she is Catholic and she is Apostolic', she identifies four ways in which these ecclesial communities are *Basic:*

> First the church is One, and the base community is a basic cell of the church. It is not a breakaway church existing as a satellite or in isolation from the main church, it is in communion with the rest of the body making it a single unity. The church is Holy, and the base communities are about the basics of Christianity of which nothing is more basic and essential than holiness: being holy and doing holy things through actions of love, sacrifice and mission. Thirdly, as the church is Catholic and universal, base communities are about the base of society, the poor, but in the base community they are regarded not as those at the bottom of the pile but are 'lifted up' so that their experience and perspective can be used to enlighten others. The very ideal of base communities reflecting the Catholicity of the church ensures that there can be no discrimination on grounds of gender, race, education or economic worth. Finally the church is apostolic, and the base community is about the base of the church, about living out the gospel concept of the priesthood of all believers; it supports the apostolate of the laity in which all members of the church, not just the clergy, have a role in the spreading of the gospel. (Dr Hebblethwaite's analysis is an expansion of *The Bare Ecclesial Church in Movement, a Pastoral Document* signed by the fifteen Mexican Bishops and Archbishops at Guadalajara in 1989.)

Margaret Hebblethwaite argues that this identification of base communities and their justification is inspired by a proper understanding of scripture and of the original role of Jesus:

> A text which is very important for people in the base communities comes from the very outset of Jesus' ministry. After he had been baptized in the river Jordan by his cousin John, called the Baptist, Jesus had retreated to the wilderness as a preparation for his life's work. While there he had been subject to specific temptations, graphically recounted in the gospel narratives. Fasting throughout

the forty days, Jesus survived these unscathed and returned to Galilee where he taught in the synagogues.

And he came to Nazareth, where he had been brought up; and he went to the synagogue, as his custom was, on the sabbath day. And he stood up to read; and there was given to him the book of the prophet Isaiah. He opened the book and found the place where it was written, 'The spirit of the Lord is upon me, because he has anointed me to preach good news to the poor. He has sent me to proclaim release to the captives and recovery of sight to the blind, to set at liberty those who are oppressed, to proclaim the acceptable year of the Lord.' And he closed the book, and gave it back to the attendant, and sat down; and the eyes of all that were in the synagogue were fixed on him. And he began to say to them, 'Today this scripture has been fulfilled in your hearing.' (Luke 4:16–21)

And the text works itself out in practice by meaning that if you are going to be a follower of Jesus you have to make your life into good news for the poor, you have to bring liberation to the people, because that is what Jesus did. He said 'Stand up and walk! Open your eyes and see! Open your ears and hear!' And I think that ceaseless witness of real physical healing showed that for Jesus religion was no 'pie in the sky' affair. If you want to be with Jesus, join with Jesus, work with Jesus for what Jesus worked for, then you have to work for real physical liberation for the poor on this earth. And this is in no way in conflict with the life beyond; on the contrary it is part of the same continuum.

But what does this mean in practice? What actually happens in the base communities? Margaret Hebblethwaite again.

I think one can see how it translates itself on the ground in communities, for example in Managua, where the communities would have all sorts of little groups attached to them, like a group working for teenage mothers, like a group who have a particular ministry to visit people in the hospital. In harder times it could mean medical help for people who were conducting an armed struggle against the dictatorship. It would mean hiding a medicine kit under the mud floors of their huts. People have shown me in their homes where the medicine kit is hidden until it is needed to tend to the wounded. Of course it was terribly dangerous to do that because if it was known that they had been giving medical aid to the people who were, for example, fighting against Samosa and his troops, they would have been killed as well. But they would simply see this work as part of their Christian commitment.

Looking to Jesus as an example of how to live your life is central to Christian belief worldwide. Christianity therefore has the person of Jesus at its heart, according to the Revd Nicky Gumbel of Holy Trinity, Brompton, the largest Anglican church in the United Kingdom and home to the Alpha course, a system of spiritual training and renewal which has proved highly successful in revitalizing individual lives and congregations across the world.

In the last two thousand years we've advanced in every field of science and technology, but no-one has ever improved on the moral teachings of Jesus, his teaching on turning the other cheek, loving your neighbour, loving your enemy, doing to other people what you would have them do to you. No-one has ever talked like that. If I was asked to sum up what it is that Christians believe, I would say it is in the two great commandments. He said the first commandment is to love God with all your heart and with all your mind and with all your soul, while the second commandment is that you should love your neighbour as yourself. In other words Christianity is not just about our relationship with God – that would be just pietistic - it is about doing something for the needs of the world around us. It is about going out and loving other people, feeding the hungry, housing the homeless, caring, praying for those people who are suffering. It is all about living your lives for other people.

Living lives for and with people is the hallmark of L'Arche Communities where helpers and people coping with mental disabilities live together in community as a family – practically supporting and caring for each other.

The first L'Arche Community was set up in 1964 when Jean Vanier, a Canadian Roman Catholic lecturer visiting France, was deeply moved by the plight of mentally retarded adults imprisoned in institutions. He bought a small house in the village of Trosly Breuil, and L'Arche began. There are now 105 such houses around the world, inter-faith communities creating opportunities for education, work situations and an interactive home life. The ethos of L'Arche is that everyone living together, handicapped persons, assistants and volunteers alike, are equal members of the community, because in one way or another each one is handicapped and a true community can be built only on the affirmation that all human beings are equal, regardless of their physical or mental state.

In their Charter, the Communities of L'Arche affirm that

> . . . each person whether handicapped or not has a unique and mysterious value. The handicapped person is a complete human being and as such he has the rights of every man: the right to life, to care, to education, and to work.

They are all inspired, says their founder Jean Vanier, by Jesus' life and example:

> The roots of L'Arche are deep in the Beatitudes and Jesus' love for, and identification with, the marginal and rejected ones of this world. Its foundations are built solidly on the granite of the gospel spirit: brotherhood, justice, truth, liberty and peace. *'Blessed are the poor in spirit... those who mourn... the meek... those who hunger and thirst for righteousness... the merciful... the pure in heart... the peacemakers... those who are persecuted for righteousness' ... sake ... those who are reviled and persecuted and calumniated against.'* (Matt. 5:3–11)

And Jean Vanier says that he is reminded of Jesus every day by those around him:

> What touches me about the people in my communities is the absolute beauty of handicapped people. Let me tell you a story of an eleven-year-old mentally handicapped boy. The time came for his first communion and there was this great occasion, a wonderful liturgy followed by a family celebration. And the uncle of the little

boy came up to the mother and said, 'What a wonderful service that was, the only thing that is so sad is that he didn't understand anything.' But the little boy overheard this and said to his mother with tears in his eyes, 'Never mind, Mummy, Jesus loves me as I am.' You see what St Paul tells us is that God has chosen the weak and foolish and despised. People with disabilities like that little boy don't want power, they don't want knowledge, they don't want money, they're not interested in those sorts of things. What they want is relationships, they want love and they want to be loved. The whole message of Jesus is compassion and to be compassionate, and showing compassion is certainly to struggle against any type or form of suffering.

Underlying Jean Vanier's work to relieve suffering – whether it is the suffering of the disabled, the homeless or the lonely – is his own personal relationship with Jesus Christ:

Jesus is an incredible lover, and sometimes he is separated from us and sometimes he is in us: that is the reality. Jesus is somebody I couldn't live without. Quite simply I wouldn't be able to live if Jesus wasn't there. My life would break up because I would become very vulnerable also.

I think when you live with people who have disabilities you let the barriers down; you don't defend yourself in the same way; you don't have projects; you don't have agendas. You let yourself be invaded. The whole message of Jesus is 'Love one another as I have loved you.' And how does he love us? He says that we are to 'live in my love'; we are to live in him and he will live in us. There's this mutuality. The whole mystery of Jesus is letting Jesus live in us so that in some way we, all of us, are the disciples of Jesus; we can become the face of Jesus, the hands of Jesus and the heart of Jesus and become the very words of Christ.

That is a vision shared by the theologian Elaine Storkey. She too looks to a personal relationship with Jesus to shape how she lives her life. There is also guidance, she says, in the stories about the life of Jesus in the New Testament.

One of the stories I love is the one where Jesus has been invited to a feast and the host is a Pharisee. It is obviously an important feast because there are important people there. But it is also obvious that these people have no real relationship with Jesus. For them he is a bit of an oddity and perhaps on show. The feast would be in the open so that there would be crowds around watching. In the crowd there is a woman watching this, and suddenly she bursts in on the assembled dinner party and quite frankly starts slobbering all over Jesus. The story is so graphic. She is weeping, she is crying, she starts mauling his feet. She handles his flesh, touches his skin. She is sobbing all over him and washing his feet. Then she breaks open this flask of perfume and starts massaging his feet. Now this is the action of a prostitute, of a woman who is into the art of seduction. And they all accuse Jesus – nudge nudge, nod nod. If this man was really a prophet he would know what sort of woman this was and what is going on here. But then Jesus confronts them, and the narrative is fascinating: the dialogue goes on like this:

'Do you see this woman? I entered your house, you gave me no water for my feet, but she has wet my feet with her tears and wiped them with her hair. You gave me no kiss, but from the time I came in she has not ceased to kiss my feet. You did not anoint my head with oil, but she has anointed my feet with ointment. Therefore I tell you, her sins, which are many, are forgiven, for she loved much; but he who is forgiven little, loves little.' And he said to her, 'Your sins are forgiven.' Then those who were at table with him began to say among themselves, 'Who is this, who even forgives sins?' And he said to the woman, 'Your faith has saved you; go in peace.' (Luke 7:44–50)

What Jesus is really saying is that this woman has made up for your rotten hospitality, so in a sense he recognizes what the woman has done, regardless of the way his hosts may have interpreted it, gives it great dignity, receives it as compensation, and tells her to go in peace. Then she talks to them about how she is so grateful because she has found in him someone who has forgiven her. And this is the other dimension of Jesus which is so important: he was someone who could forgive our sins.

And it was that claim of Jesus – to be able to forgive sins – which opened him to the charge of blasphemy.

Blasphemy has come to be understood as impious or profane talk against God, and in some western legal systems, the offence of reviling God or Jesus or the established church has been included on the statute books, but in the context in which Jesus was speaking, blasphemy was, among other things, claiming for one's self the qualities which alone belong to God – and it was clearly understood in Judaism that it was only God himself who could forgive sins. So if Jesus had claimed that power, and called himself the Son of God as well, then he would have committed blasphemy and thus be liable to punishment by death.

It is apparent from the gospel stories that it was this claim to forgive sins which disturbed the Jewish authorities most and enabled the Temple hierarchy to investigate the authority of Jesus' teaching, to take counsel together and, according to the Law of Moses, find him guilty of blasphemous talk. Any discordant teaching on the Torah would be tantamount to an attack on Israel itself which was why, when Jesus came to Jerusalem that last time, he was so assiduously questioned by the authorities.

First the chief priests and the elders came to him and asked him, 'By what authority are you doing these things, or who gave you this authority to do them?' In true rabbinic convention, Jesus responds with another question and asks them, 'Was the baptism of John from heaven or from men?' Recognizing a trap, the questioners say they do not know, and Jesus responds, 'Then neither will I tell you by what authority I do these things.'

Then some of the Pharisees and Herodians asked him if it was lawful to pay taxes to Caesar or not. In a masterly object lesson Jesus calls for a coin, identifies the head on it as Caesar's, and tells the questioners that they should pay to Caesar the things that are Caesar's but they should reserve for God those things which belong to God.

Next some of the Sadducees came and put to him the case of a woman who had been married in turn to seven brothers, each of whom had died. In the resurrection, they asked, whose wife would she be, as she had been married to each of the seven brothers? Jesus points out that 'when they rise from the dead, they neither marry nor are given in marriage, but are like angels in heaven'. This reply not only confused his questioners but has continued to perplex generations of exegetes and preachers ever since!

Finally a single scribe asked him, 'Which commandment is the first of all?' Jesus replies by saying, 'The first is "Hear O Israel: the Lord our God, the Lord is one; and you shall love the Lord your God with all your heart, and with all your soul, and with all your mind, and with all your strength." The second is this, "You shall love your neighbour as yourself." There is no other commandment greater than these.'

It is no coincidence that in Mark's gospel the account of the questioning comes immediately before the preparations for the Jewish Passover in chapter 14. 'It was now two days before the Passover and the feast of Unleavened Bread. And the chief priests and the scribes were seeking how to arrest him by stealth, and kill him.'

Because they were subject to the Roman law rather than their own Mosaic law, the Temple authorities had no power to implement capital punishment, which is why the Roman authorities had to be involved. Jesus was handed over for trial to Pontius Pilate, who was Governor of Judea at the time (26–36 CE) and charged not with blasphemy but treason ('He stirs up the people'), found guilty and subsequently executed in a Roman form of execution for crimes against the state.

His death points back to who Jesus really was, according to the theologian John Bowker:

> In the earliest hymn we know, which was composed close to the death and resurrection of Jesus, Philippians 2, they are singing about Jesus being 'in the form of God' but as not clinging on to that divine form as something to be kept to himself. Jesus comes as a servant, as one who serves even to the point of being obedient to death on the cross, and therefore God says of this human being, this is Jesus: at his name every knee shall bow. The whole creation is his servant now. Scholars and commentators have talked a lot of

nonsense about the Jesus portrayed in the pages of the New Testament. Commentators suggest that he was just another ordinary Galilean teacher who because of the power of his teaching was promoted to being the Son of God; that is nonsense. It is almost the other way around in the New Testament. The earliest writings that we have associate Jesus with God *as God* but they never let go of the fact that he was a human being as well. And by the end of the New Testament period, the evangelists are almost putting a foot on the brake saying, yes, of course he was God but don't forget that he was an ordinary human being as well, and then they go on to tell the story of how ordinary a human being he was, with accounts of human relationships, with expressions of emotion, anger, affection, concern, and with doing ordinary human things like partying and cooking.

So who was Jesus? An ordinary human being, a Galilean teacher who believed and knew in his own experience that God was mediating his own power through him in word and action. He was so sure of this that he decided he must go to Jerusalem: the word he used is *dei* in Greek – '*it is necessary* that we should go up to Jerusalem.' Why? Because the only person at that time who could decide whether Jesus was right or wrong, whether he had authority in what he was saying, was, as it says in the book of Deuteronomy, chapter 17, 'the judge who shall be in office in those days'. And this is something very important, for in Deuteronomy it states clearly:

If any case arises... which is too difficult for you, then you shall arise and go up to the place which the Lord your God will choose, and coming to the Levitical priests and to the judge who is in office in those days, you shall consult them, and they shall declare to you the decision. Then you shall do according to what they declare to you... and you shall be careful to do according to all they direct you; according to the instructions which they give you, and according to the decision which they pronounce to you, you shall do... The man who acts presumptuously, by not obeying the priest who stands to minister there before the Lord your God, or the judge, that man shall die; so you shall purge the evil from Israel. (Deut. 17: 8–12).

If the teacher who is under test still insists that his word is right and the High Priest is wrong, you must execute him – it is the only capital offence. You can't let him go on teaching because he is going to destroy Israel.

There is the story of another Galilean later than Jesus. He was taken through the courts claiming his teaching to be right, but the other rabbis disagreed and said he was in error. And this other teacher said, 'I'll prove I am right. Ask me to perform any miracle you like and I'll do it.' So the rabbis asked him to make the river flow uphill, and he did it. Still the rabbis remained unconvinced that he was a true teacher. Then this poor teacher called out to God to vindicate him, and a voice comes from heaven saying, 'Yes; he is right, the rest of you are wrong.' But still the rabbis shook their heads and said 'No – the teaching has to be protected by the majority in Israel.'

When Jesus goes to Jerusalem all the questions that are put to him are about the authority of his teaching, whether it is the question about tribute to Caesar or about the resurrection of the dead.

When he is brought, eventually, not to trial – there is no trial of Jesus in the New Testament – there is an examination of Jesus to see whether he counts as an aberrant teacher, and in the gospels the accusation against Jesus is that he is threatening the Temple. (Stephen, the first Christian martyr, was likewise executed for threatening the Temple, and stoned to death with the rabbinically trained Saul – later, after his conversion, to be called by his Roman name of Paul – 'consenting unto his death'.) So when the High Priest asks what Jesus is going to say about all this, Jesus says nothing and that is why he has to be executed. Not because he said anything blasphemous, but because he would not accept the highest authority of that time. And then the High Priest says, 'What need have we of further witnesses, we now know he is guilty' and they arrange his execution at the hands of the Romans.

That is what we know about Jesus: a teacher possessed by the sense that it is God, not himself, who comes to Jerusalem to try to share this with others, who cannot betray what has been entrusted to him from God. But this is inevitably in conflict not with the Jews, not with Judaism – there were many Jews who agreed with what Jesus was saying, many Jews who accepted Jesus as the Christ. You cannot ever say that the Jews crucified Jesus. There was no conflict between Jesus and Judaism. There is conflict between Jesus and some of the authorities in Judaism at that time because they worried about the authenticity of his teaching. But that did mean that he had to be executed and he was.

The Revd Nicky Gumbel would agree that Jesus was executed for claiming to be who he was – the Son of God. Christians believe, however, that the death of Jesus was the fulfilment of God's plan for redeeming humankind, a plan which began with the Incarnation when Jesus took human form in Bethlehem:

He came for a specific purpose which was – the word often used is saved – to set free mankind. He came to die for us. That was the purpose. Jesus said that he came to give his life as a ransom for many. He changed the whole of humankind; the whole created world would be restored as the result of what Jesus came on earth to do.

The biblical picture is that the world was created by God as good: everything about the created order was good. He created human nature as good and there is something noble about every human being. At the same time something went wrong. Every human being is, to use the theological term, fallen; everyone has sinned, done things which are wrong. And because of that, the image of God which is in every human being is marred. Jesus came to do something about that. Through his life, but primarily through his death on the cross, where he took upon himself all the wrongdoing of humankind and then through his resurrection, he enabled us to have a relationship with God. He enabled wrongdoing which had caused a cloud to come between us and God to be removed and therefore he made it possible for you and me to have that relationship. And it is out of that relationship that everything comes: freedom from guilt, freedom from addiction, freedom from death even, because the ultimate result of things we do wrong is death. And Jesus' life and death has defeated death and therefore set us free from death, set us free from the fear of death and with that all the other fears that are associated with death.

From the earliest accounts of Jesus, his role in reconciling men and women to God through his life and death has been seen as the reason that he was born as a man. Curiously the church has never codified its doctrine of Atonement but there are endless accounts of how his life, death, resurrection and ascension result in the forgiveness and reconciliation with God which, during his life, he mediated to many in his teaching and ministry.

Like so many doctrines which have become part of Christian faith, the Atonement has its roots in Jewish experience. The Day of Atonement is the most significant date in the Jewish calendar. According to the book of Leviticus, it was the day when atonement shall be made for you, to cleanse you: from all your sins you shall be clean before the Lord. Forgiveness is sought from those who have been wronged, and confession must be made. Traditionally the Day of Atonement is the day when Moses was given the second tablets of the Law and it is said that if all other feasts were to be abolished, the Day of Atonement, on which the Israelites resemble the angels, would remain. Until the destruction of the second Temple one of the more graphic traditions was to cast lots between two goats, sacrificing one in the Temple, and driving the other one out into the wilderness, carrying away the people's sins. In contemporary Jewish practice Yom Kippur is a twenty-five-hour fast devoted to prayer and worship, recollecting the sins of the past year and seeking forgiveness for them from one another and from God. At the heart of the liturgical celebration is the *Kol Nidrei* (Heb. 'all vows'). Repeated three times, it declares that all vows made rashly to God and not performed are now cancelled.

Quite simply Atonement (a word used for the first time in the sixteenth century) describes the reconciliation of sinners with God through the cross, as taught in the scriptures and practised through the sacraments of the church.

Five major theories of the Atonement exist, which can be described as objective or subjective. Each of them can be seen as coming from the Bible, but the Bible itself propounds no simple theory of or for the Atonement. It was left to theologians from different historical periods and theological traditions to emphasize one or other of the elements which are embraced in the concept of at-one-ment.

Objective theories claim that something factual has been done for humankind which it could not have done for itself. It is as if a disabled humanity has been pulled up by its own bootstraps when, because of its physical disablement, it could not achieve this on its own. It needed an external force to take the shoe strings and with inhuman strength pull humanity free from the morass in which, because of its sinful nature, it has been immured.

The penal theory claims that Jesus has borne the penalty instead of humans so that God can freely forgive sin. The sin, elsewhere called original sin, has been punished but instead of sinful humanity paying the price for its fallen state, it was Jesus, a sinless victim, who paid the price and was executed. Jesus becomes a substitute for each person.

Sacrificial theories refer to Jesus as a sinless offering who makes universal expiation of the stain of sin. Atonement is seen as a victory against evil and sin personified in the devil.

Moral exemplary theories claim that the extent of God's love revealed in Christ and especially in his acceptance of a brutal and unjust death were so great that they move us to repentance.

In the twentieth century, there was a stress on the corporate nature of atonement. The death and resurrection of Jesus are reca-pitulated in baptism and eucharist which constitute the church, the people of God, as his body. It has transferred the understanding of atonement and salvation from the exclusively personal into the social context. Through the redeeming act of Christ society has been redeemed.

But no single theory has won universal acceptance and it is fairly unlikely that one ever could. Perhaps that is the nature of the signifi-cance and uniqueness of it. The work of Christ in the Atonement is so far removed from human understanding that it is not possible to take it in its entirety. Each theory of the Atonement highlights one aspect of what Christ has done for humankind. In the end, although

Christians claim they cannot really understand it, it is part of their faith to accept thankfully 'so great a salvation'.

Perhaps John Burnaby in his book *Christian Words and Christian Meanings* (Hodder, London) helps to clarify this lack of agreement and resolution on a tenet of faith so central, so crucial to every Christian regardless of denomination:

> There never was, and there never can be, a theory of the Atonement that is worth the paper it is written on. If we want to understand God's reconciliation of the world to himself, there is nothing that we can do but listen to those who have known it as a reality in themselves. If we ask them, 'How do you know that the one Christ died for all?' – they can only answer, 'At any rate he died for me', and if we ask them how they know that, they will say with St Paul that they have known the power of his resurrection and the fellowship of his sufferings. Yet it is only too manifest that 'all' have not known that fellowship and that power; 'all' have not died with Christ and found their life renewed and strengthened by his. Once more we ask: what can it mean to speak of an atonement consummated on the Cross? Does not the world still wait to be reconciled? The only answer is that the finality of the Atonement is the finality of the Incarnation.

For John Bowker, realization of the Atonement, the saving work of Christ, brings home the reality of personal insufficiency, incompleteness:

> It makes me despair. The longer I have spent trying to understand Jesus in the Jewish context of his time, the more certain it is that he was the initiative of God, the reality of God, translated in and through human life. God was in Christ reconciling the world to himself. It is true. There is no way around it. I spent the first third of my working life trying to find ways around it, translating it into Jewish teachings and so forth, and he is not like them. The New Testament conveys an extraordinary phenomenon of Jesus making an impact on people of such a kind that they had to fall down before him and say 'I am not worthy to touch you', and yet clinging

to him because they would not let him go. And I know it is true. Look at what I do, say, the way I behave and it is hopeless, it is so far from the truth that I know and which touches me . . . and then I suppose despair is such a strong word and was what sent Judas out to hang himself . . . It can only be answered in the way that God took the initiative to reconcile us, to rescue us all – from that despair. And therefore each day although I miss the mark, which is the real meaning of what sin is, nevertheless I know that I can go back like the Prodigal Son in that great teaching of Jesus, who having taken his inheritance, has gone away and spent it all in riotous living and been reduced to working as a swineherd; he comes to his senses and argues with himself that at home his father's servants eat better than he does now, and resolves to go back and beg forgiveness and serve his father as a servant. And like the prodigal son, at the end of each day I can say, 'I have done it again, I have been amongst the pigs', and each day he opens his arms in forgiveness.

And [the son] arose and came to his father. But while he was yet at a distance, his father saw him and had compassion, and ran and embraced him and kissed him. And the son said to him, 'Father, I have sinned against heaven and before you; I am no longer worthy to called your son.' But the father said to his servants, 'Bring quickly the best robe, and put it on him; and put a ring on his hand, and shoes on his feet; and bring the fatted calf, and kill it, and let us eat, and make merry; for this my son was dead, and is alive again; was lost, and is found.' And they began to make merry. (Luke 15:2–4)

4

The Resurrection of the Body

Fundamental to Christianity is the unique belief that Jesus, the founder of what was to become this new religion, was raised from the dead on the third day after his crucifixion. Crucifixion was traditionally a Roman punishment reserved for dangerous outlaws, and the fact that Jesus, together with two other men, convicted robbers, was executed in this manner, at noon, on the day before the most important Jewish Feast of Passover further raises questions about the trials and sentencing of Jesus. Traditionally victims of crucifixion took a long time to die: while nails pinned wrists and ankles to the wood, it was the weight of the body pulling down that caused a slow strangulation. The crucified were executed in public places, and displayed on hill-tops or along the main Roman roads as examples to would-be revolutionaries or trouble-makers. Added to the excruciating pain and public abuse, the attention of vultures and the fierce sun ultimately precipitated death.

According to Jewish law, it was imperative that Jesus be dead and laid to rest before the onset of the feast (at sunset the same day), which according to John's account was also a Sabbath. St John recounts how:

Since it was the day of Preparation, in order to prevent the bodies from remaining on the cross on the sabbath (for that sabbath was a

high day), the Jews asked Pilate that their legs might be broken, and
that they might be taken away. So the soldiers came and broke the
legs of the first, and of the other who had been crucified with him;
but when they came to Jesus and saw that he was already dead, they
did not break his legs. (John 19:31–3)

It is important to notice that the Jewish authorities needed permission
from, and the help of, the Roman authorities to ensure that the
customs of Sabbath and Passover should be observed and the death of
the three victims hastened.

While historical accounts of crucifixion under the Roman Empire
exist – the execution of Spartacus and his fellow slaves rebelling
against the unjust system of slavery is well documented – no similar
accounts of corpses rising from the dead exist. The gospel narratives
leave no room to doubt that Jesus was dead, nor do they leave any
room for some hypothetical accusation that, in order to support the
so-called heretical teaching of their master, Jesus, that he would rise
from the dead, his disciples came by night to the tomb to steal the
body.

While Matthew has the fabulous account of the 'veil of the temple
being torn from top to bottom' and of tombs being opened and the
bodies of the saints who had fallen asleep being raised, he also has a
sombre account of Joseph of Arimathea, a rich man and secret disciple
of Jesus, risking his reputation and fortune by begging from the
Roman Governor, Pontius Pilate, the body of Jesus for appropriate
burial. Matthew also describes how, once the body was taken from the
cross and wrapped in a linen shroud, it was lain in Joseph's own tomb
which had been hewn from the rock and protected from predators
and grave robbers by a great stone which was rolled in front of the
opening. Matthew also describes how on the following day, the chief
priests and Pharisees came to Pilate and, reminding him of Jesus'
prophecy that 'after three days I will rise again', asked that the tomb
be sealed carefully in case the disciples should steal the body and then
compound their crime by telling the people that 'he has risen from the
dead'. But Pilate, having more important things to do with Roman
soldiers, tells the priests that as they have their own Temple guard,

they should go and make sure no-one could steal the body. 'So they – the chief priests and Pharisees' – went and made the sepulchre secure by sealing the stone and setting a guard.

Mark's account – the earliest – adds a human touch, in that when Joseph begs the body for burial, Pilate expresses surprise that the condemned man has died so quickly, crucifixion being one of the slowest forms of death, and 'summoning the centurion, he asked him whether he was already dead. And when he learned from the centurion that he was dead, he granted the body to Joseph.' Luke adds the information that Joseph was a good and righteous man, a member of the council but one 'who had not consented to their purpose and deed and [who] was looking for the kingdom of God'.

John's gospel tells us that Nicodemus, who had at first come to Jesus secretly to find out about his teaching, brought 'a mixture of myrrh and aloes, about a hundred pounds' weight, and [he, together with Joseph] took the body of Jesus, and bound it in linen cloths with the spices, as is the burial custom of the Jews.'

If it is important to see Jesus against his Jewish and Palestinian background, it is also important to see this Christian belief in the Resurrection of Jesus against the Jewish understanding of life after death. The belief that people will ultimately rise from the dead is not found in the Hebrew scriptures until the end of the biblical period, and belief in the resurrection of the dead was one of the great issues dividing the Pharisees (who believed in it) from the Sadducees (who did not). Perhaps it says something about belief in the resurrection of the dead that after the destruction of the second Temple in the year 70 CE, the Sadducees ceased to exist, while the Pharisees went from strength to strength and in many ways can be identified as the precursors of the great Rabbinic movements which have dominated Jewish thinking from the second century and are today at the epicentre of the revolution which is happening in Judaism and Jewish understanding.

But Matthew continues his narrative:

Now after the sabbath, toward the dawn of the first day of the week, Mary Magdalene and the other Mary went to see the sepulchre. And behold, there was a great earthquake; for an angel of the Lord descended from heaven and came and rolled back the stone, and sat upon it. His appearance was like lightning and his raiment white as snow. And for fear of him the guards trembled and became like dead men. But the angel said to the women, 'Do not be afraid; for I know that you seek Jesus who was crucified. He is not here; for he has risen, as he said. Come, see the place where he lay. Then go quickly and tell his disciples that he has risen from the dead, and behold, he is going before you into Galilee; there you will see him. Lo, I have told you.' So they departed quickly from the tomb with fear and great joy, and ran to tell his disciples. And behold, Jesus met them and said, 'Hail!' And they came up and took hold of his feet and worshipped him. Then Jesus said to them, 'Do not be afraid; go and tell my brethren to go to Galilee, and there they will see me.' (Matt. 28:1–10)

Mark has a similar narrative, but in his account the women are bearing spices to anoint the body (the assumption being that there would have been no time before the onset of the Sabbath), and as they approach the place, they express concern that they will not have the strength to roll away the stone. But when they find the empty tomb they see a young man dressed in white who tells them:

Do not be amazed; you seek Jesus of Nazareth, who was crucified. He is risen, he is not here; see the place where they laid him.

And the women are sent off trembling and astonished, and the gospel itself ends with the somewhat unsatisfactory and unlikely statement that 'they said nothing to anyone, for they were afraid.'

According to Luke, when the women do tell the apostles what happened, 'they did not believe them because these words seemed to them an idle tale.'

John's gospel has Mary Magdalene alone finding the tomb empty, and then running to find Peter and John, who, on hearing the news, themselves run and discover the grave clothes neatly folded, but leave the empty tomb for the safety of their homes. Mary meanwhile encounters the risen Jesus, whom she initially mistakes for a gardener and asks that, if it is he who has moved the body, he would take her to the place so that she might take it away. When Jesus turns to Mary and says her name she recognizes that it is indeed Jesus, and responds with the word 'Rabboni', which means teacher (or more accurately my teacher).

Four similar accounts, each with a different emphasis and different characters, but all in the same place in Jerusalem – a tomb cut into the rock.

In the heart of the winding streets which make up the walled city of Old Jerusalem lies the Church of the Holy Sepulchre. In spite of the aesthetic appeal of the Garden Tomb some distance away and outside of the present walled city, most Christians venerate this as the site of the death, burial and resurrection of Jesus. The first church to be built on the site was in 326 CE when Helena, scouring the Holy Land for relics, reportedly disinterred the lance with which the side of Jesus had been pierced. Persian invaders destroyed this early building in 614 CE, but it was rebuilt almost immediately, only to suffer systematic destruction again in 1009 CE when the Egyptian El Hakim employed wrecking crews who knocked down the stone walls, and took hammers and picks to the tomb itself, leaving only debris covering the area. When the Crusaders took Jerusalem in 1099, they built a Romanesque church complete with bell tower, which, in spite of regular attempts at destruction, inadequate repairs, fire and earthquake, provides the basis of the site pilgrims today venerate.

Father Jerome Murphy O'Connor from L'Ecole Biblique, who has spent a lifetime studying the archaeology of the Holy Land, describes the Church of the Holy Sepulchre:

> One expects the central shrine of Christendom to stand out in majestic isolation, but anonymous buildings cling to it like barnacles. One looks for numinous light but it is dark and cramped. One hopes for peace, but the ear is assailed by a cacophony of warring chants. One desires holiness, only to encounter a jealous possessiveness: the six groups of occupants – Latin Catholics, Greek Orthodox, Armenians, Syrians, Copts, Ethiopians – watch one another suspiciously for any infringement of rights. The frailty of humanity is nowhere more apparent than here; it epitomizes the human condition. (*The Holy Land*, OUP, 1992, p. 49)

Early on any Sunday morning visitors will be overwhelmed by the cacophony of competing liturgies which sweep around the building. In an apse made from a series of caves and supposedly the earliest part of the building, the Syrian Orthodox celebrate their liturgy in the ancient Aramaic, the language which would have been the common tongue at the time of Jesus. Just outside and behind the Sepulchre itself the Ethiopian Orthodox worship, while on the eastern side, in a recently restored apse, the Greek Orthodox outnumber the rest. Slightly later the Armenians with the choir from the Patriarchate process, singing, to the Armenian chapel, and later again the Franciscans come to celebrate the Roman Mass. For traditionally brought up Christians with their familiar liturgies, inherited assumptions about sacred sites and mental luggage, a pilgrimage can be a disturbing experience, but there is something remarkably uplifting about the fact that Christian traditions dating from the earliest community, the 'living stones' who were Jesus' followers, worship alongside every known denomination and recent religious sect in the place which represents the central fact of Christian faith, an empty tomb.

Archaeologists are keen to point out that this present site would have been well 'outside the city wall' at the time of Jesus, a significant observation because no executions or burials could take place within the precincts of the holy city.

The two foci of devotion in the church today are the tomb itself, set in the western apse and, just inside the main entrance and up a marble stairway, the two chapels of Calvary and Golgotha: Calvary, the responsibility of the Roman Catholic Franciscan friars, is to the right and marks the very place where it is believed that Jesus was stripped of his garments and nailed to the cross. In the chapel of Golgotha, all candlelight, oil lamps and silver icons and in the care of the Greek Orthodox, there is, under the altar, a bronze disc with a hole, believed by the faithful to be the place where the cross was hammered into the hilltop.

The authenticity of the Church of the Holy Sepulchre as the actual site of Christ's crucifixion and resurrection was strengthened when archaeologists dug to its foundations as recently as the 1960s. What they found corresponded with the biblical account in the New Testament. Fr Gerry Murphy O'Connor:

> Here in the courtyard you can visualize what the scene was like at the time of Jesus, for where now you can see chapels on the left-hand side of the courtyard as you enter and the monasteries on the right-hand side, there were the walls of a quarry. Inside the domed building – the Calvary – there is a piece of rock sticking out – you can actually see it – which was so inferior that the quarry men just cut around, leaving it standing. That quarry was opened in the sixth century BCE but they ran out of the stone in about the first century before Christ. So what you had here then was an open space – the stone having been removed – and what an enterprising entrepreneur did was to cut and build a catacomb in which he would sell individual graves. And when the archaeologists went down to check the foundation of the church they found earth in which were traces of figs and cereals, so we have for the first time full proof that St John's gospel is absolutely correct because he describes the burial of Jesus very simply. *'Now in the place where he was crucified there was a garden, and in the garden was a new tomb where no one had ever been laid. So because of the Jewish day of Preparation, as the tomb was close at hand, they laid Jesus there'.* (John 19:41–2)

But for many believers the place is more than an archaeological verification of what they believe. Bishop Samir Kafity, until 1998 the Anglican Bishop in Jerusalem, regularly leads pilgrimages through the old city explaining the spiritual significance of the sites. He considers the Church of the Holy Sepulchre, as do many Christians, to be the holiest site in Christendom. No-one, regardless of personal commitment or agnosticism, can visit the tomb in his company without understanding the significance the place holds for believers.

> This is the *empty* tomb where Jesus Christ came back to life after being condemned to death. This is the place where the new beginning, the new life, the new Testament was started. Here people from every nation come to pay homage and pray and worship the living Lord.

There are many cathedrals in the world with full tombs. Here in Jerusalem is the only cathedral in the world which has an empty tomb!

As a native of this city of Jerusalem, I am always reminded when I come here that the mixture of pain and glory ends up here. Glory starts from this place. I am reminded of St John who quoted Jesus saying '*I came that you might have life and that you might have it abundantly.*' We are having this new and abundant life from this very place, this empty tomb.

As we move under the low doorway and go down a step we enter the chamber where is the empty tomb. Here we enter into the innermost part of life, the innermost truth of Christianity, the innermost place of this cathedral – the empty tomb.

You look and there is no corpse. Christ is living. What you do see are worshippers, pilgrims saying their prayers, from all over the world lighting candles on behalf of their loved ones, their churches and people, kneeling saying their prayers. We are at the holiest of holies, what lies at the heart of the Christian faith.

Each Friday afternoon, Jerusalem's Franciscan friars lead pilgrims from all over the world along the Stations of the Cross on the Via Dolorosa – the name given to the devotional walk through the streets of Jerusalem that retraces the route followed by Jesus as he carried his cross to Golgotha.

Bearing in mind that the city of Jerusalem was systematically destroyed by the Romans in 70 CE when the Temple was burned and the final six thousand Jewish Zealots died in the flames or by the swords of the Roman soldiers, the present Via Dolorosa can only be an approximation of the paths walked by Jesus as he carried his cross to the 'green hill far away outside the city wall'. Archaeological investigations have revealed how thoroughly and ruthlessly Roman troops pulled down palaces, shopping precincts and elegant town houses and mansions. Even the city walls were, except for a small section, demolished, and visitors found it hard to believe that Jerusalem had ever been inhabited. The Romans were determined to warn the Jews from attempting any further rebellion against the authorities.

Although the Romans imported Syrian and Greek civilians to inhabit the desolate city, then called Aelia Capitolina, some Jews remained, and according to the third-century church historian, Eusebius, some of those Jews were 'Jewish Christians ruled by Jewish Bishops'. Such current organizations as the movement 'Jews for Jesus', an American-based group of Jewish converts to Christianity who retain the customs and practices of their Jewishness, would regard these Jewish Christians as their forefathers for, during the first century, there was a distinctively Jewish strand within Christianity: Jews who accepted Jesus not as divine but as the Messiah. They accepted him as a mere man but one who was worthy to fulfil the prophetic role outlined in the prophets and anticipated by the thinkers. Indeed on their door in San Francisco the office of *Jews for Jesus* is indicated by a name plate with the legend:

Jews for Jesus
Founded 33 AD
Give or take a year or two.

It is custom in most religious traditions for devotees to visit the tombs of their spiritual and intellectual masters, and the graves of Jewish sages and teachers, Kabbalists and interpreters of the Law, were no exception. It is probable therefore that these original Jewish Christians, in honouring the places associated with events in the life of Jesus, kept alive the knowledge of their location in the albeit desolated quarters of Jerusalem.

Today the first Station, set in a school yard, marks the place where Jesus was tried and condemned to death, while across the road, the contemplative gardens of the Monastery of the Flagellation commemorate the scourging of Jesus and the place where he 'took up the cross'. Climbing up through the old city, the third Station where, overcome by exhaustion and weakness, Jesus fell for the first time, is marked by a chapel built by soldiers from the Free Polish Forces in 1946 while a few steps further on is the fourth Station where Mary traditionally embraced Jesus. The fifth Station, where Simon of Cyrene, a visitor to Jerusalem, was forced into the indignity of carrying the cross of some criminal, is at the next corner. As the street turns at a rightangle, the sixth Station marks the spot where a woman, tradition has called her Veronica, wiped the face of Jesus and found his face imprinted on the cloth. Higher up the street is the seventh Station where Jesus fell for a second time, and then some fifty yards further on at the eighth Station is the place where Jesus, addressing the women of Jerusalem, warned them not to weep for him but for themselves and for what the future was to bring. The ninth Station, up a steep ramp, marks the place where Jesus fell for the third time.

The final Stations of the cross bring pilgrims into the Church of the Holy Sepulchre itself and up to the chapels of Calvary and Golgotha: the tenth where Jesus was stripped, the eleventh where he was nailed to the cross, the twelfth where he died, and the thirteenth marking the deposition, where he was taken down from the cross, while the final Station, where Jesus was actually laid to rest, is a cavernous, dimly-lit rotunda.

Here, if it has a geographical location, must be the locus of Christianity. This is the place which inspires the other thirteen Stations. Indeed it could be argued that this is what inspired the previous centuries of Jewish revelation, the wanderings of the patriarchs, the wisdom of the judges, the solemnity of the kings, the wisdom of the writers, the spiritual insights of those who wrote psalms, the visions of the prophets, the experience of exile, of diaspora, of return and renewal. For Christians believe that the special covenant relationship which God had established with a chosen people reached its fulfilment here. The events of this place proved God's ongoing presence with his people in a renewed, unique and quite unmistakable presence.

For what would be the point of preaching to the women of Jerusalem, of falling under the weight of the cross, of forcing a foreign tourist to become part of the sordid procession, of a towel impressed with the sweating, bleeding features of a tortured criminal, if having been laid in the tomb, Jesus had remained there, if the crucifixion, death and burial of Jesus had been the end of the story?

Christians believe that three days after his death Jesus rose again from the dead. His resurrection is undisputed by many of the pilgrims who follow the Stations of the Cross today. But what evidence is there to support the first-century biblical account of Jesus rising from the dead? For Christians the evidence is not to be found in theological argument, even in investigation, but in experience of the presence of the risen Christ in their lives.

While individual Christians and church groups are often accused of failing to reveal the triumph of the resurrection and the presence of the risen Christ in their lives and worship, there is not a church nor Christian individual who would not confirm that it is the experience of the living Lord which motivates their lives and their communities.

And to explore one such community, we move from the pilgrimage centre of early Christianity to a pilgrimage centre of twentieth-century Anglicanism, London's Holy Trinity, Brompton, the church which boasts the largest congregation in the United Kingdom. It is only yards from Harrods, an equally famous, if secular, place of pilgrimage for visitors from all over the world. The Revd Nicky Gumbel is a priest here:

> The resurrection is the lynchpin of Christian belief because the Christian faith is a reasonable faith; it is not a blind leap of faith into the unknown. It is a reasonable step of faith based on good historical grounds. It's based on the life, death and resurrection of Jesus Christ. There is very good historical evidence for the resurrection. We know that Jesus died on a cross – that is a historical fact. We know also it was regarded as the most disgraceful form of death both to the Jews, who said that a man who was hung on a tree was cursed, and also to the Romans who regarded it as the punishment reserved only for the worst criminals, people who were at the bottom of the pile. So no-one was going to follow someone who died on a cross; no-one was going to do anything in their memory. Yet a few days later a movement started that spread throughout the whole known world in three hundred years. No-one has ever found another suitable explanation for those two historical facts except the physical resurrection of Jesus which is of course supported by

the fact that the tomb was empty, that he appeared to the disciples, that they were transformed and that millions of people throughout the ages have been transformed through a personal experience of the risen Jesus Christ.

For the Revd Richard Burridge, Dean of King's College, London, an academic whose research has been concerned with the study of Greek and Latin texts of the period, it is that personal experience which provides the most convincing argument that the resurrection did take place, rather than the texts which he studies.

> Certainly for myself, speaking as a classicist, not as a Christian, I found myself saying that this claim that Jesus rose from the dead is rather important. So, looking at all the evidence and using the methods of ancient history I asked what are the theories, what is the best explanation of the fact that this movement survived when all the others did not? And I found myself increasingly coming to the conclusion – rather like Sherlock Holmes – that when you've eliminated all the impossible, what you are left with, however improbable, must be the truth. And I found myself coming to the conclusion that it looks awfully as if Jesus did rise from the dead.
>
> Now if that is the case and he's alive today, then I should be able to see him and meet him personally. And I found myself saying, 'Hey, Jesus, if you are alive, how about making yourself known to me, because if you are alive it seems to me something pretty important!'
>
> I believe that Jesus arose from the dead not from any critical analysis or academic researches, important though they are, but because my experience is of Jesus alive with me here, now and day by day.

Adding weight to that personal experience of the resurrection is the Christian belief about who Jesus actually was.

> Christians believe that Jesus was the Son of God, the source of all light and life and truth according to the writer of the fourth gospel. Now if that is the truth you can't actually kill God. The amazing thing is that Christians believe that Jesus was a human being who

came into our world and shared our life. There are other accounts of the death of Jesus which also say that God could not possibly have died. But we actually believe that God has entered so much into human experience that he wasn't afraid to experience death, and that God the Father raised Jesus from the dead on the third day.

What actually happened? Well we have stories: the women going to the tomb in the early hours to anoint the body of Jesus, because they had not been able to do it on the eve of the Sabbath, and when they got there finding it empty. Then of course you can start thinking of all sorts of reasons why it might have been empty: grave robbers were a common problem in the ancient world. There were all sorts of issues about whether they went to the wrong tomb in their distress, and so forth. But the amazing thing is that the more one looks at these theories they become even more unbelievable than the extraordinary thing that Jesus did rise from the dead. It is very unlikely that the disciples would have stolen the body and then turned round and preached that Jesus had risen from the dead!

Keith Ward suggests that as the penalties for preaching the resurrection were severe in the extreme, the disciples would have been unlikely to fabricate evidence.

In the gospels if you ask why the apostles should be trusted, I do think you have a number of choices here; one is that they were lying. Well, I suppose that it is just possible, but you have to remember that some of them went to pretty horrible deaths for what they said and so that is not too plausible an explanation. Could they have been deceived? But consider their teaching – and I think you would have to look at their teaching – it seems to be of an extraordinarily high moral worth and literally world-changing, spiritual power. And, although it is possible that this could be founded on deceit, it doesn't seem a very probable hypothesis. So if you are to ask why should the apostles be trusted, I would root that in the moral power of their lives, the nature of their charismatic renewal, in the ways in which their whole lives became more self-giving, and in the fact that they recorded and passed on to the community and had written down in the gospels later, some of the facts and some of the sayings of Jesus which are actually very diffi-cult for them. They didn't just pick up the bits they liked – there are all sorts of difficult passages. But that's perhaps a very deep ques-tion, an ultimate question as to whether one can accept the Christian faith or not.

Do you trust the apostolic witness to the resurrection? I can understand people who say, 'I am not sure, they might have been deceived.' Because I think I share with lots of other Christians what I take to be a personal experience of Christ as alive and as conveying the presence of God, I think that personal experience is the final weight, which leads me to trust the apostolic witness.

For John Bowker, there are two great arguments supporting the authenticity of the resurrection.

The first is that the records of it are so chaotic. There is no well-worked out account as though the disciples, the witnesses, had a good story to tell in order to make more converts. Religion is big business; if you want to make a great impact, maintain a high profile, then run a crusade and convert people. The stories of the resurrection are not told like that, so the first major argument that the resurrection happened was that something hit the disciples and took them by surprise. They were not expecting this. They under-stood that the Son of Man had to die – they had seen him die on the cross. But the Son of Man as the one who will be vindicated beyond death, as described in the book of Daniel, they had not got that! He had died on the cross, but if their expectations had been fuelled by the picture in Daniel, there would have been legions of angels, the sea boiling over; it would have been mountains splitting and extraordinary things happening. But it was none of those things – it was a man standing in a garden and he was mistaken for the gardener. Although it took them by surprise, they were sure it was him, although it was not exactly like the 'him' they had known. He seemed to pass through doors and appear and disappear in a way he never did during his life on earth, but still there was a recognizable continuity from the one they had known from his life on earth while it was not exactly like him.

The first thing you cannot say about the resurrection is that it was mass hallucination – no way. The second thing you cannot say is that as the result of his teachings and work and ministry they decided as an act of preservation to say, 'Well, he was a great teacher; we don't want his teachings to disappear so we shall just say that he is alive, we'll call it a resurrection!' That will not do; it's not true. In the Jewish context the vindication has to have sufficient substance, it has to be sufficiently real in form and bodily presentation, and that is what they saw.

The second major argument for the resurrection is that almost instantly his followers are talking about Jesus in ways they talk about God.

As good Jews they knew what belonged to God alone: the forgiveness of sins, the rule of the cosmos, creation, but all these things become associated immediately with Jesus as God. So the second major argument for the resurrection as something that truly happened is that they start to talk about this Jesus, the man who had died, in ways they talked about God. This is not something which came later. The earliest writings we have are immediately talking about Jesus as God.

It was the belief that the Jesus who rose from the dead was the Son of God that immediately marked out the early Christian faith as a religion distinct from Judaism – Jews don't accept that Jesus was the expected Messiah and don't acknowledge that Jesus rose from the dead. Richard Burridge again:

Christianity has its genesis in the Jewish tradition and faith. Jesus was a Jew, his followers were all Jews, and our belief in God is rooted in the Jewish scriptures and their understanding of God as Father Almighty, the Creator and so on. But the genesis of Christianity as a separate movement comes out of the resurrection, because the resurrection is God's vindication of Jesus of Nazareth and the separation of Christianity from its Jewish parent, though it would be better to talk of development out of the multi-cultural setting of first-century Palestine which included all sorts of different cults: the Essenes, the Sadducees, the Pharisees, the Christians within the first century would all have been seen as groups within first-century Judaism. It is only really after the Jewish War of 70 CE and particularly after the Jewish rebellion of 132–5 CE that you have what we now understand as Rabbinic Judaism and Christianity which both, as it were, come from it, and the point at issue between Rabbinic Judaism and Christianity after the destruction of the Temple in Jerusalem in 70 CE was the nature and person of Jesus of Nazareth: whether or not he was God's Messiah, whether or not he was raised by God. The resurrection is therefore the genesis of Christianity because it is the focus of the discussion that took place between the Jesus movement and other similar movements which did not accept the Christians' claim for Jesus.

As well as various accounts of an empty tomb and of various of his followers encountering Jesus or an angelic presence there, the gospel writers describe a number of independent appearances which Jesus made to his disciples in different locations and at different times over a forty-day period before he was, according to Matthew's gospel, finally taken up into heaven.

In Matthew, Jesus meets his disciples and instructs them not to be afraid but to go to Galilee where he will appear to them. Apparently some remained unconvinced but nevertheless went to Galilee where Jesus meets them and commissions them to:

> Go therefore and make disciples of all nations, baptizing them in the name of the Father and of the Son and of the Holy Spirit, teaching them to obey all that I have commanded you; and lo, I am with you always, to the close of the age. (Matt. 28:19–20)

Luke recounts how two followers of Jesus, one named Cleopas, the other unnamed but in the light of the story probably one of the original disciples, who are going to the village of Emmaus, some seven miles from Jerusalem, fall in with a stranger who seems ignorant of the great events of the previous days:

> 'Are you the only visitor to Jerusalem who does not know the things that have happened there in these days?' And he said to them, 'What things?' (Luke 24:18–19)

Their account of the trial and death of Jesus whom they had been led to believe was the long-promised Messiah, and the stranger's knowledge and interpretation of the prophetic utterances concerning this expected Messiah last until they get to Emmaus, where they invite the stranger for a meal, during which he 'took the bread, and blessed and broke it'. It is by this action and the words used that the two recognize their fellow-traveller as Jesus, but *he vanished out of their sight*. The language Luke uses is the same as that used in the institution of the Eucharist, the Last Supper, when, in the context of the Passover meal, Jesus 'took bread, and when he had given thanks, he broke it and gave it to them saying, "This is my body".' That Jesus should disappear before completing the meal and before blessing and sharing the wine can be interpreted as a fulfilment of his words at the Last Supper when after he had taken the wine cup he said to the disciples, 'Take this, and divide it among yourselves; for I tell you... I shall not drink of the fruit of the vine until the Kingdom of God comes.'

Returning to Jerusalem, they find eleven other disciples gathered, and no sooner have they told them what has happened than Jesus himself appears to them, and to assuage their fear that he is a ghost, asks for food and eats it before them. He then leads them out to Bethany where, having blessed them, he disappears from them.

John's gospel, the latest to be written, brings together a number of stories about Jesus' post-resurrection appearances, each used to illustrate some theological point. He appears to his disciples and invests them with the Holy Spirit and bestows upon them the power either to forgive sins or to withhold such forgiveness. Alas, Thomas was not there at the time, and when told by the other disciples of the appearance he remains cynical and exclaims:

> 'Unless I see in his hands the print of the nails, and place my finger in the mark of the nails, and place my hand in his side, I will not believe.' (John 20:25)

Eight days later, Jesus re-appears to them and gives Thomas the opportunity to prove to himself that the apparition really is the Jesus who was crucified and whose side was pierced with a lance.

Then Jesus appears to the disciples who, fed up with inaction, had decided to revert to their old business of fishing. But a night on the Lake of Galilee produces nothing until a stranger on the shore instructs them to cast their net once again on the right side of the boat. Inevitably they trap an enormous catch which proves too much for the nets to hold, whereupon John identifies the stranger and says to Peter, 'It is the Lord', and Peter impetuously swims to the shore while the other disciples drag the net – now full of fish – ashore.

A fire has been prepared, and Jesus asks for some of the fish they have caught, and prepares breakfast for them. He then takes the opportunity of asking Peter three times whether he really loves him and, being assured that Peter does indeed love him, instructs him in turn to 'feed my lambs', to 'tend my sheep' and 'feed my sheep'. Jesus goes on to warn Peter that although strong and able now, and master of his own destiny, there will come a time when he will need help to dress himself or to work, and others will force him to go where he does not want to go. The writer adds that this is a warning to Peter of his forthcoming martyrdom.

Each of the stories recorded, although containing some conflicting internal evidence, has significant theological importance for the future of the church. In Matthew the dominical command to proclaim the gospel, the story of Jesus, to all nations, baptizing them and making them Christians, has been the inspiration for and despair of Christian missionary outreach. In Luke, the Emmaus encounter and recognition is put into a eucharistic context, paralleling the words of Jesus to his disciples on the night in which he was betrayed and which encapsulate the basis of all eucharistic liturgies, while in John, Thomas's doubt enables Jesus to tell his disciples that they are indeed blessed, because having seen, they believe, but how much more blessed would be future followers who believed without ever having seen (either, more immediately the wounds themselves, or more generally, the person of Jesus).

These stories of a post-resurrection Jesus prove problematic not only in the narrative of the gospels but also for Christian belief. They belong more to the genre of apocryphal gospel than the sober

accumulations of miracle stories, of sayings and comment that make
up the rest of the gospels. So if the early Christians claimed that Jesus
had risen from the dead what did they actually mean had happened?
Did they believe in a resuscitated Christ into whose dead body new
life had been breathed? How *did* they see him when he appeared to
them after his death? Keith Ward suggests that it was not in recognizable human form:

> In the gospels, the resurrection is actually portrayed not as the
> appearing of an ordinary flesh-and-blood body among the apostles,
> but rather more in the way Paul was later to describe it in his vision
> as a body of light which indeed was often difficult to recognize.
> This person walked for seven miles without being recognized, so it
> was not an ordinary human body. I think the gospels do not tell us
> that Jesus got up and walked away from the tomb and went and hid
> somewhere in Jerusalem except when he talked to the apostles.
>
> They talk of the disappearing of the body from the tomb; it had
> ceased to exist, and they talk first of an appearing of Jesus behind
> locked doors and then a disappearing. What they are describing is a
> series of visionary appearances. The gospels speak of these as real;
> they are neither hallucinations nor illusions. It is not as if a body
> opened the door and walked in and then said, 'Where is the number
> 9 bus down to Gethsemane?'
>
> It is rather that there was an appearance of the glorified body of
> Christ among the disciples which could then cease to appear, in other
> words a visionary appearance. That I think is what the gospels say,
> and that is what Paul is so strongly affirming when he says 'flesh and
> blood' – the ordinary stuff – 'cannot inherit the Kingdom of God'.

But in whatever form the risen Christ appeared to his disciples, it is his
Resurrection that remains the central belief of Christianity. Without
it, the faith doesn't make sense, according to Kenneth Bailey, the
former Professor of New Testament at Jerusalem's Ecumenical
Institute:

> The New Testament presents about eight different pictures of ways
> to understand the crucifixion. One of them is the image of the great

battlefield where a battle is engaged. What we are talking about is the great battle between sin and death, and the response to that in the scriptures is that there is victory over sin and death which is the resurrection. If there is no victory and no resurrection then we have to look at the death of Jesus as we look at the death of Socrates, a great man who died for what he believed, an enormous loss, and think of all we could have had if, like John Kennedy and so many others, he had not died young.

To make sense of the Resurrection, Kenneth Bailey says, it is vital to look first at the Crucifixion and why Jesus died on the cross. For him the crucifixion and resurrection are two sides of the one coin and can best be understood in the parables – or stories – Jesus told his followers: parables like that of the prodigal son.

Think in terms of the great story of the prodigal son, the boy in the far country – we are told that after some time he wants to go home, but in going home he thinks he will keep the rules. He has lost the family inheritance. He thinks he is going to work in the family fields. He thinks he is going to work as a hired servant and gain enough money to pay back what he has already spent. But the real issue is not the keeping of the law or the making up of his losses in the terms of the law. The real issue is that he wanted his father's inheritance when his father was still alive, which in Middle Eastern terms and culture means he wanted his father to die. So here he has caused his father the agony of rejected love. He cannot make up for that by working hard. This is a different kind of a problem. The father, at the end of the story, runs down the road to welcome him, while he is scared of whether or not he is going to be welcomed at all. This unexpected and costly gesture of love makes a reconciliation which he can't make even if he works for thirty years and pays back every penny. You insult me in public today and tomorrow you say, 'How many dollars shall I write the cheque for?' – that's not the problem. The father says he was dead and is alive, he was lost and is found, meaning that, at the edge of the village, he was still dead and lost and I, through this costly demonstration of love, have reconciled him to myself. Jesus sees himself as that figure. He is the one who in the name of God, demonstrating the presence of God in the community, is offering costly love to reconcile the human race back to love.

And that takes us back to Creation and the Fall. In Christian terms that love offers a solution to the problem of our alienation from God which happened right at the beginning, in the story of the fall of mankind in the book of Genesis. Having been alienated – this is represented by the prodigal son in the far country – we are now reconciled, not because we manage to get ourselves home, but because God in Christ comes to us and, with a costly demonstration of love, reconciles us to himself.

And this central message, this love in action, is what marks out Christianity as being different. It is not so much the question of the Resurrection, it is the question of this divine presence in the person of Jesus who through this act of costly love reconciles us fallen human beings to himself. This is what lies at the heart of the Christian faith, and is in essence all that Christianity is about.

This is what Christians call the Atonement – the belief that by his death Jesus could redeem our sinful nature, restoring the original relationship between God and his creation. Elaine Storkey of the Institute for Contemporary Christianity:

Many Christians, and I am among them, believe that Christ's mission on earth was not just to show us a good way of living but theologically it was bound up with actually taking us through the pattern of sin into forgiveness and to what is called redemption. It was part of God coming to buy back the creation which was already his. That's why I think the term redemption is such a helpful term. In Victorian England you redeemed something if you went to buy back something you had given to the pawnshop owner in exchange for a loan. It was yours all the time; you just needed more money to buy it back than you had been loaned in the first place. So we have a picture of redemption as God coming to buy us back from sin, from bondage, which the Bible describes it as, or slavery, from that inability to be in a good relationship with God. The resurrection comes to show us that it is completed: we have been bought back for God and can live an eternal life.

It was the Resurrection of Jesus, then, that gave substance to the belief that there could be eternal life – in other words life after death.

> I think the real reason he rose from the dead was not only to show that he had won victory over death, or to show that death, which was the last enemy, was not going to defeat him, but also to give us hope that we too would rise from the dead. But from the human point of view it also shows us that we need not fear death.

And that is a reality for many Christians today – Christians like Joel Edwards, the General Director of the Evangelical Alliance in the United Kingdom, an organization which acts as the representative body for all evangelical Christians, regardless of any denominational allegiance, to promote evangelical unity and truth and to represent evangelical concerns to the government and in the media.

> The Resurrection says that ultimately nothing is impossible for God. The Resurrection is actually the heart of hope, so the Resurrection says that even in death God is able to make a way out. So death itself, the great terror of all human beings (250,000 people die every day), is no longer a terror because of the Resurrection, so it vindicates God's sovereignty over death, that which humans fear above all else.

For Christians like Joel Edwards, Christianity is unthinkable without the fact of the Resurrection; it could never have survived as a movement, let alone developed as perhaps the greatest religious movement in history. In fact he argues:

> I do not think that Christianity would have been born if we did not have the Resurrection. The Resurrection was what the disciples preached, it was the thing they lived, and furthermore the Resurrection made sense of life and work for them here. So there was a correlation, a relationship between what we do here and the Resurrection. For example, when Paul talks about life beyond this world he links it powerfully with our deeds here. The Resurrection does not say we qualify for life after death because we did good deeds, but good deeds only ultimately make sense in the light of the

Resurrection. I think it is because of the Resurrection that I am able to make sense of what life is all about here, and for me the power of the gospel, all the things which God claims to give us in Jesus, life, begins now. It is about a quality of life which is not based on material things. It is about a quality of life which is not limited to what we have or we don't have, a quality of life and a value of life which helps me as a person make sense of the senselessness of life. So that kind of infusion of reality coming from the ultimate reality of life beyond here, of the power of the Resurrection, is for me quite an important stone in my Christian experience.

And it also gives meaning to life on this earth according to Elaine Storkey:

Erich From once described human beings as the freaks of the universe; we have all this potential, all this energy, all this power, all this longing inside and then we die, it all comes to an end, and it is all pointless ultimately. And therefore Christianity at the heart says it's not pointless because it continues with us wherever we are; whatever we've been, whoever we are, continues in a refined way into the next life.

Few of the ancient religions, whether Semitic or Asiatic in origin, which have survived, have any belief that there will be anything like a heaven or a hell, either a worthwhile life with God after death or a punishment after death. The idea developed very late in human history. This means that human belief in God is an extraordinary human fact, far more sensational than the discovery of the wheel or fire, or even of splitting the atom! Our ancestors discovered the truth and reality of God without any belief that it was going to do them any good; it was not going to lead them to a reward or a punishment after death. They served God, worshipped God for God's own sake simply because God was a fact, a reality. They eventually came to believe that if God is in relationship with us in a relationship of encouragement, of love, of correction, then maybe he continues that relationship after we have died. He created us in the first place, maybe he can go on with this after death. So belief in the continuity of relationship with God has come in to all the religions

in some form or other. But the point is not the place of this continuity or the description of its nature, it is the affirmation that the
truths that they discovered before they believed that there was any
life after death are so true that they want to go on affirming them
now.

If God is like this in my life here and now, maybe there is a way in
which it will continue after death. What is different about
Christianity is its belief that God took the initiative in Jesus to bring
that trust and creativity and love and correction and encouragement into the midst of human life, into the language of human life
and then took all that reality through death into the Resurrection
and caught us up on the sort of whirlwind which that created, and
carries us up with him through that Resurrection so that our life
with him is not destroyed by death but continues.

The reality of the next life is how many Christians make sense of this
life and the suffering or difficulties it may bring. Kenneth Bailey was a
lecturer at the Near East School of Theology in Beirut during the
Lebanese Civil War:

> I think of a good friend of mine who was my colleague in Beirut
> before he returned to Germany; he was Dutch in origin. As a Dutch
> Christian he had joined the Dutch Underground and ended up in
> the death camps, but survived them. One night he told me his story.
> And after the story, which took two hours to tell, I said, 'Joe, how
> do you keep your sanity?' And the simple answer was that beyond
> the cross is the Resurrection. We ourselves as a family survived
> twelve years of the Lebanese civil war and it was that dynamic,
> regardless of what horrible days one lives through, in the dynamic
> of the Christian faith there is the cross and then there is the
> Resurrection. An American black preacher has put it very simply.
> 'Yes. it is Friday but Sunday is coming!' So whatever we suffer,
> whatever hard days we go through, this is not life's ultimate ques-
> tion. Here is a paradigm which enables us to go on and discover the
> wonders of Easter morning after the long Good Friday.

This Christian belief in the Resurrection is particularly central for
Kenneth Bailey and his family, and his conviction that it is the Easter

Sunday experience which follows on the darkness of Good Friday is a personal reality:

> Our son has a brain tumour and the doctor tells us he has two years to live. I am 67 and death is not too far from me. We will not lose him, we will be together in the Resurrection.

In such experience faith is tested and tried, and in the witness of such certainty comes the inspiration for what Christians do believe.

5

The Holy Spirit

Set just a stone's throw from fashionable Knightsbridge is the church of Holy Trinity Brompton. Two and a half thousand Christians come through its doors to worship every Sunday and it has a lively programme of events throughout the week. Members of the church believe its growing popularity is explained by the power of the Holy Spirit at work reviving Christianity throughout the country. But what is this Holy Spirit and what do Christians believe about ways in which manifestations occur today?

In Holy Trinity Brompton the Holy Spirit, it seems, is often present in a very physical way. For one of its senior staff, the Revd Nicky Gumbel, that is not unlike how the Holy Spirit first appeared to the early Christians in Jerusalem almost two thousand years ago at the feast of Pentecost, originally called in Hebrew Shavu'ot (meaning weeks). The Hellenists preferred to use the word Pentecost (Greek for fiftieth day) because it was celebrated fifty days after the feast of the Passover and traditionally marked the conclusion of the barley harvest and the beginning of the wheat harvest. More interestingly in the light of its significance for Christians, it became – in later Judaism – the day for celebrating the revelation of the law to Moses. Because the crucifixion of Jesus occurred immediately after the Passover – indeed John's gospel compares Jesus to the sacrificial lambs which were slaughtered for the feast – and the Resurrection took place on the day after Passover, the church celebrates this coming of the Holy Spirit, Pentecost, fifty days after Easter. Frequently referred to in Christian calendars as Whitsunday, it was traditionally a day when Christians were baptized; the title comes from the white clothes which newly initiated Christians would wear.

> When the day of Pentecost had come, they were all together in one place. And suddenly a sound came from heaven like the rush of a mighty wind, and it filled all the house where they were sitting. And there appeared to them tongues as of fire, distributed and resting on each one of them. And they were all filled with the Holy Spirit and began to speak in other tongues, as the Spirit gave them utterance. Now there were dwelling in Jerusalem Jews, devout men from every nation under heaven. And at this sound the multitude came together, and they were bewildered, because each one heard them speaking in his own language. And they were amazed and wondered, saying, 'Are not all these who are speaking Galileans? And how is it that we hear, each of us in his own native language? Parthians and Medes and Elamites and residents of Mesopotamia, Judaea and Cappadocia, Pontus and Asia, Phrygia and Pamphylia, Egypt and the parts of Libya belonging to Cyrene, and visitors from Rome, both Jews and proselytes, Cretan and Arabians, we hear them telling in our own tongues the mighty works of God.' And all were amazed and perplexed, saying to one another, 'What does this mean?' (Acts 2:1–12)

For Nicky Gumbel, as for many Christians, such manifestations of the Holy Spirit are not limited to the pages of the Scriptures:

> As you read that account in the book of Acts, about that day of Pentecost, you read that there were manifestations of the Holy Spirit, which are described as being like 'tongues of fire', or like 'the roaring of a mighty wind from heaven'. I think people today still have these physical manifestations just like the tongues of fire on the day of Pentecost. Sometimes people feel enormous heat rushing through their bodies, or they feel as if the wind is blowing upon them.

On the day of Pentecost people started spontaneously speaking in another language, one that they hadn't learned. Again, that is one of the things we find now. Sometimes as people experience the Holy Spirit, they start to praise God in a language which they had not learned before. It might be a recognizable human language or it could be the tongues of angels, a language which is not recognized and cannot be identified.

Speaking in tongues or *glossolalia,* a term coined in the nineteenth century, is identified by psychologists as the abandonment of conscious control of the speech organs to the subconscious. Some people have believed the resulting speech to be divinely initiated, and in the course of revivalist movements within Christianity it has played a prominent part, most notably today in the Pentecostal Movement and in Charismatic Renewal. It is a phenomenon which from its outset has been regarded with caution by many Christians and critics alike.

St Paul, the first Christian writer to comment on glossolalia or the gift of tongues, is always careful to qualify its use, almost to limit its power, and to warn people that it is a useless charism or gift unless there is someone who can interpret the sounds and make sense of them.

> *Now, brethren, if I come to you speaking in tongues, how shall I benefit you unless I bring you some revelation or knowledge or prophecy or teaching? If even lifeless instruments, such as the flute or the harp, do not give distinct notes, how will anyone know what is played? And if the bugle gives an indistinct sound, who will get ready for battle? So with yourselves; if you in a tongue utter speech that is not intelligible, how will any one know what is said? For you will be speaking into the air.* (1 Cor. 14:6–9)

In the famous poem of love in the same letter to the Corinthians he writes:

> *If I speak in the tongues of men and of angels, but have not love, I am a noisy gong or a clanging symbol.*

In the light of recent experiences of the Charismatic Renewal

Movement, which have frequently been marked by an emphasis on the exercise of the spiritual gifts, it is easy to understand Paul's stress on the need for an accompanying gift of interpretation alongside the more dramatic and obvious gift of speaking in tongues. Spiritual superiority was not a problem just for the early Christians, and one of the tensions caused by the Charismatic Movement has been the division between those who manifest such charismatic gifts and those who do not. Paul, the well-trained rabbinical scholar and Roman citizen, is aware that enthusiasm needs to be disciplined by reason and logic: the spirit matters but so does the mind. Unfortunately, some modern-day charismatics have failed to observe Paul's guidelines and instead have used their experiences to divide the faithful into apparent 'first class' and 'second class' citizens.

> *He who speaks in a tongue should pray for the power to interpret. For if I pray in a tongue, my spirit prays but my mind is unfruitful.* (1 Cor. 14:14)

And this ability to interpret or translate the languages or tongues is a phenomenon the Revd Joel Edwards is familiar with. For him, speaking in tongues, together with their interpretation are true signs that the Holy Spirit is at work, and he remembers vividly one such manifestation during a church service:

> About ten years ago in a worship context I had a quite profound experience. An eight-year-old-girl, who had been born in England of Jamaican parents and had obviously never ever studied any other languages, started speaking in a language which evidently was not her mother tongue. And there was someone at the meeting who was able to interpret what she was saying. The following day I saw the person who had been interpreting what the girl had been saying, and I said, 'I didn't know that you had that gift of the interpretation of tongues.' And she said, 'I don't have any spiritual gift for the interpretation of tongues.' And I said, 'But you were interpreting what the girl was saying last night.' And she said, 'I wasn't interpreting, I was just translating because that eight-year-old-girl was speaking perfect French.' It was quite amazing.

Now we know these kind of phenomena belong to the reliability of the New Testament documents. In the letter to the Corinthians, one sees those kind of things but this was not in the first century, this was now! And when you can see that gift operating in the context of worship throughout the world, then you put a marker down which tells you that there is coherence between what the Bible says about the work of the Holy Spirit in the believer and what you experience now in the twenty-first century. The manifestation of these gifts marks the continuity in two thousand years of Christian experience.

The theologian, Elaine Storkey has been the director of the London Institute for Contemporary Christianity, an organization which explores the relevance of the teachings of Christ for the experiences of today's world.

People argue in the Christian church a lot about whether what happened at the Feast of Pentecost when all those disciples spoke in different tongues and gave prophecies and produced miracles was just for the day of Pentecost itself or whether it was to be part of the church's work for today. Well I think the jury is out on it, frankly, but I do believe that a lot of what we see which is of a supernatural nature are genuine manifestations of the Holy Spirit. And it is not just in the British church, it is in the church world-wide. It is a far-reaching phenomena, seen particularly, perhaps, in Africa and parts of Asia far more than in Europe now. And the reason that I think that they are genuine manifestations of the Holy Spirit is because of what follows them. Usually there is repentance, a change of heart towards God and towards one another. I think miracles still happen within the church. I think there are healing miracles which still take place. I think people do have prophetic utterances so that they can see the truth of a situation in spectacular new ways. So yes, I do believe that the Holy Spirit continues to manifest himself in this kind of way. But that does not mean that every single instance that is reported is actually the work of the Holy Spirit. It could also be hysteria!

That was an accusation levelled against many churches affected by the so-called Toronto Blessing, which started in January 1994 in a small charismatic congregation of the Vineyard denomination in Toronto in Canada and has spread around the world during the last decade of the twentieth century. The congregation of the 'Airport Vineyard' experienced what they believed to be a completely new outpouring of the Holy Spirit not just on an occasional Sunday service but night after night, as people flocked to what has become famous worldwide as a renewal centre inspired by the manifestation of the Holy Spirit.

Congregations caught up in it found that their members would not only speak in tongues and have visions and prophesy but would fall to the floor, or begin to shake or giggle or laugh uncontrollably. The effect of the Toronto Blessing has been felt around the world, particularly in the mainstream denominations of the United Kingdom, South Africa, East Asia and North America. The movement has not been without its critics, but nonetheless individuals who have experienced it claim spiritual refreshment, a personal encounter with God, a new love for Jesus and a commitment to the mission of the church.

For Keith Ward, Regius Professor of Divinity at Oxford, the Bible lays down clear guidelines for identifying whether such dramatic and supernatural experiences are indeed of the Holy Spirit:

> The Holy Spirit and the work of the Holy Spirit is best set out, I think, in one little sentence in St Paul's letter to the Galatians in the New Testament where it speaks of the fruit of the Spirit as being *'love, joy, peace, patience, kindness, goodness, faithfulness, gentleness and self-control'* (Gal. 5:22). So the marks of the Spirit in Christianity ought to be seen in expressions of that compassion and kindness and love. Those are the most important things that the Spirit brings. As Paul goes on to say in Galatians, *'and those who belong to Christ Jesus have crucified the flesh with its passions and desires. If we live by the Spirit, let us also walk by the Spirit. Let us have no self-conceit, no provoking of one another, no envy of one another'* (Gal. 5:2–6).
>
> There are other phenomena which people exhibit and I would not deny that they may be produced by the Spirit, but unless they are subordinated to the pattern of love then you often have to be

very suspicious about the way in which people can take their ability to do strange paranormal things as the work of God. The test is, are these works of love? Are these works of the compassionate Jesus Christ or not? Given that, I think one might even *expect* that the Spirit would be revealed in extraordinary outpouring, especially from time to time.

But the works of the Holy Spirit do not start with Pentecost; they have a long history. In the Jewish Scripture the Spirit is the breath of God that 'broods over' the chaos which was before creation and from it brings order. Throughout the Jewish Scripture the Spirit is seen not as separate from God but rather one of God's ways of working. It was the Spirit which enabled Saul to prophesy to the band of prophets at Geboah; it enabled Samson to kill the lion: 'he tore the lion asunder as one tears a kid and he had nothing in his hand' at the vineyards of Timnah. The Spirit was what marked out the prophets from other men and women and gave them the power not only to discern the meaning of events but to look to the future. In the later prophecies the Spirit is seen as divine action in the final judgement when God will pour out his spirit on all flesh. 'Your sons and your daughters shall prophesy, your old men shall dream dreams, and your young men shall see visions' (Joel 2:28).

It was believed by later Rabbinic commentators that the Holy Spirit had been withdrawn from Israel at the time of her exile to Babylon in 597 BCE, as part of the punishment for her failure to maintain a pure Judaism and avoid assimilation in the face of Assyrian occupation. This exile marked the end of the classical age of prophecy in Judaism and with it a change in ways in which the Holy Spirit could be discerned. Without the recognized office of prophet, wider claims to inspiration were made which, in turn, would prepare for a later recognition of its manifestation in the work of Jesus himself.

Keith Ward suggests that with Jesus, the Holy Spirit's activity took on new dimensions, and his work and words consciously pointed the minds of contemporary observers and thinkers back to the work and words of the prophets.

In the Old Testament, the Spirit of God is said to inspire the people who designed the Temple, the people who wrote psalms, those who went and fought in bloody battles, so the Spirit is a great power and energy which transports people beyond themselves. In the New Testament Jesus is said to have sent the Spirit upon his followers in a new way. It was the same Spirit, the same creative energy of God, but now it appeared in a new way because it was the Spirit of Christ. It had taken the form of Christ in the lives of the apostles. But again it had the same effect, energizing and inspiring. It was God working throughout the whole universe and through human hearts. And after Jesus, the Spirit comes to convey the character and nature of Jesus Christ to human beings so that they can shape their lives on that pattern.

The work of the Holy Spirit then is clear, it is manifested in specific ways which result in moral and spiritual improvement of believers. But what or who is the Holy Spirit?

The earliest writings which refer to the Holy Spirit are those of Paul in the New Testament who identifies the Spirit with the risen Christ:

Now the Lord is the Spirit, and where the Spirit of the Lord is, there is freedom. (2 Cor. 3:17)

In the gospel of John, Jesus promises his disciples that after he has gone away from them they will receive a counsellor, a comforter, sometimes called the Paraclete – a direct transliteration of the Greek word – whom he identifies as the Holy Spirit.

'I will pray the Father, and he will give you another Counsellor, to be with you for ever, even the Spirit of truth, whom the world cannot receive, because it neither sees him nor knows him; you know him, for he dwells with you, and will be in you . . . These things I have spoken to you while I am still with you. But the Counsellor, the Holy Spirit, whom the Father will send in my name, he will teach you all things, and bring to your remembrance all that I have said to you.' (John 14:16–17, 26)

While the official credal definition is that the Holy Spirit is the third person of the Holy Trinity, distinct from but co-equal with the

Father and the Son and in the fullest sense God, it took the early church some three hundred years to agree upon the words they should use to explain what they thought the Holy Spirit was. To explain its activities they produced the doctrine of the Trinity – the idea that God exists as three persons in one – the Father, the Son, and the Holy Spirit.

According to the American Lutheran, Lora Gross, the Christian church's theology has been glaringly deficient in setting forth a detailed doctrine of the Spirit. For her, the Spirit is understood as the divine purpose and intent coming to fulfilment through humans in the transformation of culture from one era to the next. The identification of the Spirit as the third person of the Trinity declares God to be the ground of the world and of life within it, and it is the Spirit which sustains the world and natural life in it. Her understanding of the notion of the Holy Spirit as the affirmation of the God-world relation in the Trinity is one with which Elaine Storkey agrees:

> The Holy Spirit is the third person of the Trinity – it is the Spirit of love, of truth, of peace, of justice, so in a sense the Holy Spirit is the embodiment of all those central characteristics of God that we know to be true, and therefore is the one who brings those characteristics to us – that is why they are called the fruits of the Spirit, that when we live with the Spirit we actually get to know these characteristics in the depths of our own being in a much more personal way because they are personified for us by the Holy Spirit. So the Holy Spirit is someone who moves around, speaks to us, acts between people, brings us to wisdom and understanding – 'enlightens our mind' is a New Testament phrase – sometimes just helps us to see things clearly in a way which we hadn't before. So the Holy Spirit is God but he's that person of God who is always moving between people and bringing them to a greater understanding of who Jesus is. I think the central work of the Holy Spirit is to show us who Jesus is and then through that, to make us different people.
>
> I think the Holy Spirit is often the least understood member of the Holy Trinity, but that is in the nature of the Spirit himself.

For the Revd Richard Burridge, Dean of King's College in London, the power of the Holy Spirit is its activity in history and relationships.

> The role of the Spirit is to draw men and women to God. There's something almost self-effacing about the Holy Spirit. The gospel according to St John talks of the way in which the Holy Spirit will convict, draw people to Jesus and to the Father, and there is almost a process, or a movement in the life of God, in that God the Father loves us so much that he sends his son, Jesus, to be with us. He so loves us that he pours out his Holy Spirit on Jesus and it brings us all in them to the feet of God, the throne of God. These are all anthropomorphic terms, speaking of God as a person, and God is, of course, far more than that. But therefore the Holy Spirit never seeks to glorify himself but always to glorify God, so it is quite understandable that Christians know, as it were, the least about the Spirit. But every time we open ourselves to God, pray to God or worship God, we are living in the life of the Holy Spirit and the fellowship that all Christians believe that they share in, the common life of the Holy Spirit.

For Joel Edwards of the Evangelical Alliance, the Holy Spirit plays a very pragmatic role in Christian life; it is the uniting force which gives to Christians worldwide a common identity and coherence.

> The Holy Spirit's involvement in our walk with God insists that we do not regard ourselves as isolated units of belief but that we recognize that each one of us is actually a part of the whole, and part of that movement of millions of people who all share the same experience in all cultures and races and nations and so on. The Bible tells us that it is by the Holy Spirit we are put into one body, into one family and so it is not at all unusual to go to different parts of the world, and to meet people from different parts of the world, and recognize a sense of belonging even though you are different and come from different places and cultures. Immediately you come to recognize that this thing you have experienced is an experience common to millions of others. So no-one privatizes this thing and hides it in a corner. It actually belongs to the family of faith.

If Christians worldwide, then, are united by the Holy Spirit, is the Holy Spirit unique to Christianity? Keith Ward again:

> Many religions have the idea of an energy, a dynamic power of God which is very often conceived of as feminine. Śakti, for example, in Indian religion, is a feminine principle manifested as a goddess and the consort of the god Śiva; it is she who is able to bring things into appearance. Wisdom in the Old Testament is also feminine; she is described as 'a co-worker with God' in the process of creation. My private heresy is that the Holy Spirit is always feminine but I don't think that will catch on, but it is a fact that this energy, creativity and power of compassion and sympathy and wisdom which is associated with the Spirit can be found in many traditions. What is distinctive in the Christian view is to associate the Spirit with Jesus, so the pattern of the Spirit always has to be conformed to the life of Jesus, which was life of healing, forgiving, compassion, reconciling, serving, love. So it is not a spirit of barbaric energy, it is a Spirit of compassionate love. But the idea of a Spirit is practically universal.

But what does that mean for Christians today? Nicky Gumbel of Holy Trinity, Brompton would argue that personal experience of the Holy Spirit is central to being a Christian.

> The Holy Spirit is described in the New Testament sometimes as the spirit of Jesus. Sometimes people describe him as Jesus' other self. He is the way in which Jesus is present with us now. He is the way in which Jesus Christ himself indwells a person. People sometimes use the expression, or talk of, 'asking Jesus into their lives'. What they are actually doing is inviting the Holy Spirit to come and live within them, so as Jesus comes to live within a person he begins to change them into his likeness. That is why they become more loving and more peaceful. That is the fruit of the Spirit.
>
> It comes about as a process; it is a relationship primarily. The Spirit of God enables us to have a relationship with God through Jesus Christ, and it is that relationship which changes things. Just as any relationship changes who we are – we are changed by the relationship we have – so a relationship with God through Jesus Christ

in the power of the Holy Spirit changes our personalities and our characters and develops them into his likeness.

One of the ways Nicky Gumbel says that he has seen thousands of people transformed by the Holy Spirit is through the Alpha courses which originated at Holy Trinity, Brompton and are now one of the major agents of renewal within the Christian church worldwide.

The need for some outreach arose out of the awareness that there were many people with a spiritual hunger who had no contact with any church, and the accompanying realization that the church had been ineffectual in reaching out to these people and getting them 'within sound of the gospel'. Holy Trinity pioneered the first Alpha course in 1979 when Charles Marnham, a priest on the staff of the church, began looking for a means of presenting the basic principles of the Christian faith in a relaxed and informal setting as a way of reaching out to people. His aim was to enable them to discover the power of God, revealed in his Son Jesus Christ through his Holy Spirit in a way that allows them to explore in an unthreatening atmosphere of love and acceptance.

The Alpha course is a fifteen-session, ten-week practical introduction to the basics of the Christian faith designed primarily for non-churchgoers and new Christians. There are talks about the person of Jesus, others on the Holy Spirit or the Resurrection. All are after a shared meal and are followed by discussion in small groups. Nicky Gumbel stresses that no question or doubt is too trivial, threatening or illogical to be considered, and every question is addressed courteously and thoughtfully – and no-one is pestered if they choose not to continue with the course. It's all friendship-based: no knocking on doors, little advertising, but friends bringing friends. It has proved a successful formula with the hundreds of people coming to every Alpha course Holy Trinity, Brompton organizes.

Perhaps it would be more accurate to describe Alpha not as a course but as a renewal phenomenon as, beginning with the five courses held in London during 1992, there were 10,500 Alpha courses held all over the world in 1998. It is not an exclusively Anglican experience: Baptist, Methodist, Roman Catholic and Church of Scotland congregations have all experienced the renewal of the Holy Spirit as the result of the courses. For Nicky Gumbel, now chaplain to Alpha, its phenomenal popularity and success is due to the Holy Spirit:

We've sensed the work of the Holy Spirit behind the Alpha course, both in our own courses and beyond. We found numbers growing so rapidly with people from outside the church coming along to find out more about Jesus. Our numbers have grown so rapidly that we regularly get six hundred on every one of the three courses we run each year. In 1993, we put on an Alpha conference here at Holy Trinity for church leaders who wanted to do something similar in their own churches. To our amazement over a thousand church leaders signed up from all over the country. They went back to their own churches and started running the course and found the same thing happening: people who were not Christians, people who were unchurched were having their lives changed. Since then we have run conferences for over thirty thousand church leaders and in this country we have 4500 churches registered with us and there are another 6500 registered worldwide for running the course, and we think that can only be the work of the Holy Spirit making it all possible.

When asked what he meant in attributing the phenomenal success of the Alpha course to the work of the Holy Spirit, Nicky Gumbel pointed out that such results could not have been achieved by human effort; the Spirit of God had to be behind such a success. The Alpha phenomenon is, he believes, something that God himself is blowing along and making possible by the power and inspiration of his Holy Spirit.

There are Alpha courses in inner-city parishes and in rural communities, while the course has been adapted for use in schools, the police force, the army, civil service and government offices as well as for businesses and in homeless projects. And for Nicky Gumbel the proof that this is indeed the Holy Spirit at work is the way people's lives have been changed after they've attended an Alpha course.

Some of the people who come on the course will come as drug addicts, or with their marriages in a mess; all sorts of things are going wrong in their lives and the Spirit will give them the power to break free from drugs, the desire to be reconciled with their wife or husband, the ability to forgive and build a new relationship within the family, and a desire to go out and to do something about the hungry, the poor and the homeless. These are just some of the ways the power of the Spirit manifests itself in human lives. What we see are people who are unchurched coming to faith in Jesus Christ, being filled with the Holy Spirit, getting excited by Jesus Christ and going out and telling their friends. That is why each course tends to grow – because they go out and tell their friends. But they also go out and do a lot of other things. One person has set up work here amongst families who have members HIV positive, particularly working with the children who are in those families. Another person will go and work in prisons, setting up an Alpha course in a prison.

Alpha now runs courses in forty-seven prisons in the United Kingdom – there's even an Alpha wing in one prison where inmates can study and pray together.

Seeing a change in the lives of people in prison has also been the experience of Cecil and Myrtle Kerr. In 1974 they set up the Christian Renewal Centre in Rostrevor – a small town near the border between the north and south of Ireland – as a place of prayer, renewal and reconciliation.

I see the work of the Holy Spirit in so many ways, but one which springs to mind in particular is the people who have themselves been consumed by hatred and bitterness over many years. Some of them have taken up paramilitary activities and been involved in many violent ways. Now, often released from prisons where they discovered that Jesus Christ is their Lord and Saviour, their lives have been transformed. Now they are working to build bridges of hope to help bring about reconciliation in Northern Ireland. I think that is obviously a work of God's Holy Spirit in their hearts.

As well as running Alpha courses at Rostrevor, there are Bible teaching, daily prayer groups, healing services and a worldwide prayer chain praying for peace in Ireland. The centre works for reconciliation between Protestants and Catholics and among those impacted by over a quarter of a century's violence. Myrtle Kerr says that it is all work inspired by the Holy Spirit, the same spirit that gave her and her husband the vision to found the centre twenty-three years ago and guided them through the smallest detail of making it possible.

> For one thing, we learned to bring every detail of the project to God in a way one doesn't necessarily do when things are provided in the normal way and you are paid a salary. In the first place we needed to pay for this large house we were buying. God had asked us to provide a place and showed us where the place was to be, and as we prayed together with friends a promise came. A young man said, 'God will put it into the hearts of the right people to give the right amount at the right time to buy this large house and to sustain the work.' So we took that as a word from God and believed that God would do that – and absolutely true to his word he did. We simply sent out a small leaflet to friends asking them to pray and setting out the work God wanted us to do. By the end of the first six months, the first instalment of £8,000 was due on the house, and all the money was raised by that date, and the same thing happened when it came time to pay the second instalment for the house. At the end of December in 1974, the amount due was another £8000 and we had precisely £8001.60 in the bank. So God is at work through the Holy Spirit in very real ways, communicating with those who are willing to hear him.

For Cecil Kerr, the power of the Holy Spirit at work is often seen in the personal life and witness of individual Christians, often those who have themselves suffered:

> The other thing that we have found here again and again is the remarkable grace of forgiveness in the hearts and the minds of people who have suffered indescribably in the violence of the last thirty years. I am thinking of one man who had a bomb put in his car: when he switched on the ignition he was blown into the sky with the explosion. He told us that as he was being taken to the

hospital, he could hear himself uttering the words, 'Father, forgive them, Father, forgive them,' like the words Jesus spoke from the cross. Harry was taken to the hospital but they couldn't do anything to save his legs, they had to be amputated at the thigh. For the months he was in the hospital he was an inspiration to all the people there, and he comes here, as he has done ever since the accident, on his artificial legs, to help and encourage the people in Enniskillen where eleven were killed and many injured. When he stood up and spoke words of love and of forgiveness and of peace, it was a medicine to the people in their own grief and sorrow. People like that inspire us and they of course are inspired by the Holy Spirit.

But how do Christians then believe that they have access to the Holy Spirit? Some clearly experience it in the paranormal, but most others say that it is through prayer and reading the Bible. Elaine Storkey, however, thinks it would be wrong to assume that there are certain hard and fast rules on how to gain access to the Spirit:

It would be almost wrong to think of God out there and us needing access, much like a password on a computer to which God then responds. I see God as always taking the initiative. So whether it is God the Father, the Son or the Holy Spirit, he is already there waiting and ready to tap into us and take the initiative. So how we do it is just to pray. We open ourselves to the possibility of encountering God, and God is already there waiting to be encountered. This is such a relief that we don't have to go out of our way to find God, we don't have to struggle to find God, we don't have to go through this wrestling to gain access to the Holy Spirit. The Holy Spirit is here now in our conversation and we can turn and appropriate the gifts of the Spirit every time we want to. It is through prayer in the technical way: you sit down and open yourself up to God. Being open to God means that you have automatic access to the Holy Spirit.

Joel Edwards believes that the Holy Spirit is crucial in enabling people to communicate with and to speak to God:

Any Christian you speak to, regardless of how long they have been a Christian, will always tell you that we sometimes hit those points where it is just difficult to articulate what is in your head or on your heart. But the Bible tells us that when we don't know what to pray for, or how we should pray, the 'Holy Spirit makes intercession for us', he arbitrates for us in ways which we ourselves sometimes cannot fully appreciate or understand but we will know that he has done that.

But let me say something which I also think is vital to Christian faith. Because the Bible says that it is by God's Spirit that we become aware of the sonship with God, there is something in the witness of the person, in the spirit of a person, which relates to the Holy Spirit, which says that you belong to God. This is not so much in ways which are privatized, hidden or esoteric and mysterious and so on, but something which actually helps you through the harsh realities of everyday experience, and also gives you the capacity to carry the vitality of your faith to others.

Many Christians would say that the last decade saw a worldwide revival of Christianity inspired by the Holy Spirit. Certainly the latter half of the twentieth century saw an emphasis on an awareness of the 'gifts of the spirit'. The Charismatic Renewal Movement spread from North American Protestant churches in the 1960s bringing a profound sense of power to traditional churches. The Roman Catholic church, not traditionally known for manifestations of enthusiasm in its liturgies, in the 1970s developed its own charismatic wing which affected and renewed liturgical celebration, expanded the understanding and use of music in worship and the role of the laity in an otherwise clerically-dominated church. By 1980, the Charismatic Movement had become one of the main lay movements within the Roman Catholic church and was recognized as such by the Vatican.

Elaine Storkey of the London Institute for Contemporary Christianity suggests that this rise in charismatic, Spirit-inspired movements is not uninfluenced by the date. One movement which has existed within the Christian church since its earliest days has held the belief in a future millennium, a thousand-year rule of Christ on earth. The belief is based on a section in the Revelation of St John, the last book of the Bible, which is concerned with the end-time. The

Revelation of St John the Divine, to give the book its full title, was written at a time when the church was undergoing one of its periods of persecution.

> *Then I [John] saw an angel coming down from heaven, holding in his hand the key of the bottomless pit and a great chain. And he seized the dragon, that ancient serpent, who is the Devil and Satan, and bound him for a thousand years, and threw him into the pit and shut it and sealed it over him, that he should deceive the nations no more, till the thousand years were ended.* (Rev. 20:1–3)

I think that towards the millennium there was a new movement of the Holy Spirit. I found it very exciting in some of the churches just seeing the buoyancy of the people: the youthfulness, the youthful nature of belief. Now in some Latin American countries the church is young in age in terms of the people there, and full of experiences that the European churches have become really very unsure about, and we feel very old in comparison. So I think this is there but what is important is that it matures and does not just stay experiential, because once the church starts haring off after experience – even experiences of God – they actually miss the very heart and nature of Christian belief, which is a day-by-day plodding on a very ordinary walk with God. He is there, but we need to pray for more maturity in the church world-wide, and I am sure we will see it.

6

The Life Everlasting

'And I believe in the resurrection of the body and the life everlasting.' The creed ends with two of the most uncompromising statements. It makes the most incredible claim about what happens after a person dies. Unlike many of the other elements of Christian belief which trace their origins to Judaism, this belief owes little to Jewish belief and practice. There was no common acceptance of life after death in Judaism, but a tradition grew up in the third and second centuries BCE that 'friendship with God' (as Abraham's relationship with God was described) might be continued by God through death. During the Maccabean period there grew up a group who considered that in the light of Israel's experiences in exile and during the period of Greek oppression, there had to be some sort of redress for the sufferings of God's chosen people. Although belief in a life after death was part of the teaching of the Pharisees, it was far from an accepted Jewish teaching about death at the time of Christ. Death itself was seen as final and as an act of judgement. However, belief in life after death received non-negotiable reinforcement from the appearance of Jesus among his followers after they had been witnesses to his death on the cross and his burial.

While Christian theologians have proved articulate in writing about most of the clauses of the creed, words have often failed them in their attempt to verbalize this final tenet. They have always found 'the resurrection of the body and the life everlasting' the most difficult to write about.

In his letter to the church in Corinth Paul addresses the belief that, like Jesus, members of the Christian community would rise from the dead. He writes:

> *But someone will ask, 'How are the dead raised? With what kind of body do they come?' You foolish man! What you sow does not come to life unless it dies. And what you sow is not the body which is to be, but a bare kernel, perhaps of wheat or of some other grain. But God gives it a body as he has chosen, and to each kind of seed its own body. So it is with the resurrection of the dead. What is sown is perishable, what is raised is imperishable. It is sown in dishonour, it is raised in glory. It is sown in weakness, it is raised in power. It is sown a physical body, it is raised a spiritual body.* (1 Cor. 15:35–8, 42–4)

He goes on to compare the first Adam with the second Adam, Jesus: one from earth and dust, the other from heaven and spirit, one a living being, the other a life-giving spirit. But the first can be transformed through the second.

> *Just as we have borne the image of the man of dust, we shall also bear the image of the man of heaven. I tell you this, brethren: flesh and blood cannot inherit the kingdom of God, nor does the perishable inherit the imperishable. Lo! I tell you a mystery. We shall not all sleep, but we shall all be changed, in a moment, in the twinkling of an eye, at the last trumpet. For the trumpet shall sound; and the dead will be raised imperishable, and we shall be changed. For this perishable nature must put on the imperishable, and this mortal nature must put on immortality.* (1 Cor. 15:49–53)

And when that happens, says Paul, death will lose its sting and the grave will be denied its final victory because, although Jesus died and was buried, it was by his resurrection that he overcame both death and the grave. This is perhaps Paul's most persuasive writing and, inspired by his earlier training as a Pharisee, reveals unquestioning faith in life after death. (It was the Pharisaic party who cut themselves off from the good things of this life in the assurance that their discipline would be rewarded in a future life.)

At a pastoral level, clergy preach homilies for weddings and christenings, confirmations and other rites of passage that are fairly predictable, but for a funeral the homily is different. In the other cases the change of status has been an experience shared by most in the congregation, the implications of the rite of passage have been explored, the formalities are known.

The baby, already part of a human family, becomes at her christening part of the family of God. Parents and godparents make promises, but so do the rest of the congregation; she becomes part of the wider responsibility of God's family. At a wedding the bride moves from one status to another, as does the groom, both assuming new responsibilities with fairly defined roles and a fairly predictable outcome. But funerals are different. We declare belief in the resurrection of the dead, but it is not something that anyone in the congregation has experienced. The so-called 'near-death experience' may have given some of the congregation insight into what they think it means, but the resurrection of the dead is not an experience shared by anyone in the congregation.

While theologians have found it hard to put into words what they understand as the resurrection of the dead, representational artists have found ways of expressing the concept of the resurrection of the body, and none more effectively than Stanley Spencer. His great series of paintings for the Burghclere Memorial Chapel show the realistic and fleshly resurrection of soldiers taking place amid the bloodbath of the First World War in Macedonia where he served with the Infantry. The place where the Resurrection takes place

is called Kalinova, where I spent the happiest time I had during the whole war. Soldiers are portrayed as handing their crosses in (symbolic of the experience that on being demobilized, one handed in one's equipment meaning that in the resurrection they have even finished with that last piece of worldly impedimenta).

Meanwhile his *Resurrection at Cookham* shows ordinary people from the town rising from their tombs in the churchyard, where graphically 'graves yawn and yield up their dead', watched by the painter and his brother-in-law Richard Carline.

John Donne describes the graveyard as being the 'holy suburb of heaven'. When it comes to why and how I came to concentrate so much on the subject of Resurrection, I think I can explain. My wish is to reveal the meaning of things . . . and I begin to search for the means of doing this. And . . . this search brings me to the contemplation of the Resurrection . . . And then I, full of hope, think, 'And what might the life be like?' There are many things in this life that I love and that I feel are for ever loved, and these things are a key to the Resurrection.

In this life we experience a kind of Resurrection when we arrive at a state of awareness, a state of being in love, and at such times we like to do again what we have done many times in the past, because now we do it anew in heaven. And so in the Resurrection there are the same beloved human ways and habits.

He wrote of his paintings of the Resurrection:

All the time you will notice a wish to emphasize the meaning in the resurrected life by giving it some link with this life, showing some sort of familiarity; . . . in each part of this picture the meaning of the Resurrection is conveyed by bringing people into contact with their customary surroundings and how they feel about them in their resurrected state. (Quoted in *Stanley Spencer at War*, Richard Carline, Faber and Faber, 1978)

One of the greatest attempts to write about the process of death and the resurrection of the body into the life everlasting was the work of the poet Cardinal Henry Newman in *The Dream of Gerontius*. Perhaps its familiarity and popularity owes as much to the work of another artist, the composer Edward Elgar whose Christian faith inspired all his music, and whose devout Catholicism influenced its structure and expression. The progression of the soul in classical Catholic belief from physical death, particular judgement (the common belief of Catholic tradition that at the moment of death the soul receives illumination which reveals itself in relation to God), through the trials of purgatory and into the realm of bliss, accompanied the while by an accommodating guardian angel, has a comforting sound to it. Elgar's music reflects the stages from fearful anticipation, through terror to calm acceptance, until the final truth of the Resurrection dawns on Gerontius, that not only is he redeemed but he will live for ever, fulfilling what Christians believe to be their most important function, the praise and worship of Almighty God: 'Praise to the Holiest in the Height, and in the depths be praise, in all his works most wonderful, most sure in all his ways.' A confirmation of Christian triumphalism against all odds and a reflection of the writer's belief in the resurrection of the dead and as the natural consequence of that belief, life everlasting.

While death does mark the end of this stage of earthly life for all, Christians profess this belief in a life *after* death. And while it is perhaps the most difficult Christian doctrine to define or discuss, theologians with few exceptions have accepted that there is life after death.

One such exception is Don Cupitt, an Anglican priest and lecturer emeritus in the philosophy of religion at Cambridge University. Don Cupitt is one of Britain's most radical theologians, the inspiration for the Sea of Faith network, a group who question the beliefs most Christians hold as central to their faith – beliefs like the existence of life after death.

> Giving up the idea of life after death is most important for the development of a modern radical theology. Many people hold on to a ghost of the idea of a life after death in order to postpone their own relationship to this life. They hold on to the hope that there will be some sort of reward hereafter, some sort of revelation of truth hereafter and then they postpone everything to that imaginary future. I would rather people discovered eternal life now rather than had a mere hope that it might be coming after death.

Keith Ward finds it hard to understand how you can call yourself a Christian and not believe in life after death:

> There's one thing I do think that Christians do agree upon and that is that, because of the resurrection of Jesus, resurrection is what

Christians hope for. But this resurrection will be as Paul says in 1 Corinthians 15: not these bodies brought back to life again but new spiritual bodies. Paul calls them new incorruptible bodies, new sorts of bodies, but there will be a communal existence in which we know other people, in which our personalities will be developed but will continue to exist, and that communal being will be free of evil and suffering and be in the presence of God. That is resurrection and that is what all Christians hope for.

For Christians like Professor John Polkinghorne, an Anglican priest and theoretical physicist, it is this belief in life *after* death, that enables him – both as a scientist and as a Christian – to make sense of this world:

Of course scientists can peer not only into the past but also into the future, and they can see in broad terms where the universe is going. And I am afraid the answer is that the universe is going to end badly! We don't quite know how it is going to end because there is a sort of tug-of-war going on between the big bang pushing matter apart and gravity pulling it together. If gravity wins, the universe will end in a sort of collapse. It will all fall back into a big crunch, a cosmic melting pot. If expansion wins it will keep on going, falling apart for ever and ever getting colder, and that way the universe ends in a sort of whimper. Either way the universe is ultimately condemned to futility. It is not going to happen tomorrow, it's not going to happen for tens of billions of years, but it is one of the surer predictions of science that in the end all will prove futile in terms of the unfolding of the present process. Now that is a very serious scientific prediction which we should take on board and to which religion has to respond. How does that fit with the claim that God is a God of purpose which is working out within the world? Well, my answer would be along these lines: I think the death of the universe on a time scale of tens of billions of years doesn't pose frightfully different problems from the equally certain knowledge of our own deaths on a time-scale of tens of years. Mortality is part of this present creation and there is no evolutionary optimism, as we can see from the unfolding of twentieth-century history; everything will not become wonderful, the Kingdom of God won't come in just like that. If there is a hope either for us or for the universe beyond death, and I believe there is, it doesn't lie in what science can tell us about present process, it lies in what religion can tell us about the faithfulness of God. And I believe that there is a hope for the universe beyond its death, just as I think that there is a hope for us beyond our death, because I think God will resurrect both. He will give a new life to the old creation. The old creation is dying but God has already begun a new creation. As a Christian, I believe in Christ's resurrection. God has already begun the work of the new creation. And that will be the fulfilment, so that is the Christian hope. But it lies not in science but in the faithfulness of God.

To look towards the end of the world in millions of years and to see it resurrected is one thing; that is objective and impersonal, but what are the implications for human beings who are in a relationship with a whole network of similarly concerned and confused human beings for whom the only certainty is imminent death?

What do I believe will happen after I die? I have first of all to say what I think the soul is. I don't think the soul is a sort of spiritual bit of me which will be liberated from the prison house of the flesh. I think I am a unity, and I think the soul is the real me, the real me is the pattern, the immensely complex information-bearing pattern, in which my body is organized. After all, the material of our bodies is changing all the time. I have very few atoms in me that were there a few years ago – that is changing but the pattern remains the same. That pattern is the soul. That pattern will be dissolved at death but I believe that it will be remembered by God, held in the divine mind, and then will be recreated, reconstituted, resurrected in fact in this new creation of God's choosing beyond death.

Not all Christian scholars have that sense of divine inevitability and the security of molecular reconstruction. The Revd Richard Burridge, Dean of King's College, London, less certain about what will happen to him, has a strong conviction that whatever happens after death, there is a continuity in relationship both with God and those he has known and loved in this life.

To talk about what happens after death, where do we go, or when do we go, is actually quite difficult because it is outside the constraints of time and space; all that the New Testament seems to tell us is that those who have died 'rest in the Lord'. They are at peace with God and that at the end of all things when time and space are wrapped up into the purposes of God – in one sense it will be for those who died two thousand years ago or those who will die two thousand years hence – in one sense it makes no difference because God is outside of time and space. And yet in another sense there seems to be an overlap of the ages in the New Testament whereby it talks of the saints – those who are with God – somehow involved in what is going on, viewing what is going on, and so on. And for me it is important that some of the great Christians of the past who have inspired me, people like St Francis of Assisi and the great saints of our tradition on the one hand, and those other saints who are known to nobody else but have inspired me, people like my grandmother, somehow are with God and somehow are praying for me and are with me. More than that it is very hard to explain but it all flows out of an idea that God loves us, we love each other, and I can't conceive of my love for them ceasing just because they have died. How much more, therefore, will the love of God go on. So whether you talk about it as all our personalities, all our memories being written in the memory of God, or whether you talk about our files being downloaded into the great computer, or being recreated in God's new existence, I don't know, but it is to do with being held in the love of God.

Some Christians believe that they are initiated into that love through paranormal experiences when they die – such as passing through tunnels with a bright light at the end and then finding themselves in a light-filled room, or that they are collected from this earth by their loved ones and safely guided into the next world. For Una Kroll, the Anglican theologian and doctor, death is to be 'the final healing'.

Whatever happens when we die, wherever we go and in whatever form we exist, Christians believe that after death there will be a time of judgement, and this belief that God passes judgement on the lives

of his human creatures is important for Christianity. This understanding of the process of judgement comes from a number of scriptural sources – from the sayings of Jesus himself:

*For the Son of Man is to come with his angels in the glory of his
Father, and then he will repay every man for what he has done*
(Matt. 16:27)

from the first history of the church:

*And [Jesus] commanded us to preach to the people, and to testify
that he is the one ordained by God to be judge of the living and the
dead* (Acts 10:42)

from the earliest writings of Paul to the embryo churches:

*Why do you pass judgment on your brother? Or you, why do you
despise your brother? For we shall all stand before the judgement
seat of God; for it is written, 'As I live, says the Lord, every knee shall
bow to me, and every tongue shall give praise to God.' So each of us
shall give account of himself to God* (Rom. 14:10–12)

and from the latest apocalyptic writings found in the Bible:

*Behold, I am coming soon, bringing my recompense, to repay
everyone for what he has done.* (Rev. 22:12)

All people will be judged, both the living and the dead, both Christian
and non-Christian, and this future judgement is associated with
Christ's final coming. While judgement will not be according to
works, it is a person's works that will provide the evidence of whether
a living faith is present in him or not. It is not a question of earning
salvation by good works, but works are evidence of the reality of the
faith through which believers are saved. But the final judgement will
be a moment of division between those who are truly revealed as
belonging to Christ and those who are not. This is no arbitrary impo-
sition from on high; the verdict of the final judgement will underline
and make known the self-judgement which men and women have
chosen during their present lives. The criterion by which people's

destinies will be determined are best understood in their relationship – or non relationship – to God.

The judgement is perhaps one of the most divisive elements within Christianity. Throughout the church's history images of the Great Assize, the separation of the sheep from the goats, the damned and the saved, did much to control and discipline individuals and communities. In modern thinking and iconography it has lost much of its power, but it does safeguard the truth that judgement is serious, just and inescapable but it is judgement by Christ himself.

The Revd Joel Edwards is uncompromising in his understanding of this judgement and the implications it has for non-believers:

> Judgement is, after all, deeply based on scripture. All Christians are fairly clear about a number things:
> One, that there is life after death.
> Two, that there is accountability after death.
> Three, God is the one who will exercise that accountability.
> Four, that as a result of that accountability there is a heaven for those whose behaviour and conduct is according to the words of Christ and for those whose faith in Christ was mediated through the cross of Christ, or in other words those who accepted the work of Christ. And for these people there will be an experience called heaven, and for others there will be an experience called hell.

Elaine Storkey is confident that there will be a judgement, not only because that is what the Bible says, but for her it is a matter of personal accountability:

> I think there are going to be questions put to us: we are going to be accountable. There are questions which are put to us every day; we are accountable for everything that we have done when we go before the face of God in prayer each evening and ask forgiveness for the things we have screwed up on, or made a mess of, or deliberately destroyed or distorted. I think the Last Judgement, if you like to call it that, is a time of final accountability where we might see things that we have missed, where God has seen things we have been self-deluded about, where there is a whole range of things we

have never confessed and never faced up to and which we will have to face up to. Sometimes it is a terrifying picture you get in the Bible of all our thoughts being revealed.

More recently, scholars have considered whether divine judgement can be seen in the events of history. John Bowker believes that judgement or accountability is happening now on this earth before death. He reflects on Gehenna, the name given to hell in the gospels according to Matthew and Mark. *Ge Hinnom,* the valley outside of Jerusalem, became a symbol for condemnation because child sacrifices had been offered there (and at the time of Jesus it was the municipal rubbish dump).

> Judgement certainly is happening now and all the time, and it is certainly given pictorial language with heaven as a place with lots of glass and lights and base-weighted dolls bobbling up and down and music, and hell is a picture of fire. We understand why these pictures came into being. Hell is *Ge Hinnom,* the valley of Hinnom which became the municipal rubbish dump near Jerusalem. The one thing you certainly don't want is to die and not have anyone remember you, the worst fate you could have is that your body was taken out and dumped on the municipal rubbish dump with no funeral rites, no-one remembering you. The municipal rubbish dump is the place where worms never die, they're always wriggling about. If you go to any local rubbish dump you can see it steaming because of the internal combustion within the dump. That's where the pictures of hell came from.

Hell has been identified as destiny, the final destiny of those who are rejected at the judgement. Christians have had many pictures of hell – from places of eternal fire and damnation to descriptions like that of the great twentieth century Christian writer C. S. Lewis who saw hell as 'a little grey town lost down a crack in the floor of heaven'. John Bowker has his own definition:

> Hell is the word we use to describe those who have ceased to be in connection with anybody: with other humans, with God, probably even with themselves. Here we are talking in terms of hell as people

who are atrophied – like all visions of hell this is only a picture – they don't have feeling, they don't have connections with others, they are in hell for ever.

That is the meaning of redemption. They are surrounded first of all by the Love of God in Christ who came to restore connections between people, connections between people and God, and then they are surrounded by the communion of saints. That's why we must always pray for other people because that is the way we enlarge the circles of love and draw people back into the circles of love .

And those who most need the prayers are those who are furthest from feeling. So does it sound ridiculous to say one must pray for people like Adolf Hitler? Of course you must pray for people like Adolf Hitler, because Jesus came into the world to reach those who act in the most cruel, vicious, thoughtless and ugly ways and win them back into relationships of love. That is the meaning of the Communion of Saints; we are won back from our atrophy into a relationship and love once more. But do I believe that it will happen for everyone? I hope it will happen for everyone because I hope it will happen for me.

Such universalist hope has not always been the currency of Christian theology. The concept of division between life and death, between those who are guided to salvation and those who are not, while never explicitly declared in the Hebrew scriptures, is, like so much of Christian theology, implicit in the thinking of the writers. When Moses intercedes with God to forgive the Israelites who had constructed an idol in the form of a golden calf at the very time he was on Mount Sinai receiving the ten commandments, he implores God, 'But now, if thou wilt forgive their sin – and if not, blot me, I pray thee, out of thy book which thou has written' (Ex. 32:32).

The later writing in the book of Daniel, set at a time of the persecution of the Jews by Antiochus Epiphanes (168–165 BCE) has even stronger resonances. Written to encourage a persecuted group, the last chapter refers to the final battle between good and evil:

> At that time shall arise Michael, the great prince who has charge of your people. And there shall be a time of trouble, such as has never

been since there was a nation till that time; but at that time your
people shall be delivered, everyone whose name shall be found
written in the book.' (Dan. 12:1)

There are references to many of those who have been killed in the
persecution and 'sleep in the dust of the earth, awaking some to everlasting life, and some to shame and everlasting contempt'.

The concept of selection and predestination came early to
Christianity. In the records of Jesus' teaching some suggestions of
predestination are present. Jesus explains to his pushy disciples that
while they might want to reserve special seats next to him in the
Kingdom of God, any such decision does not rest with Jesus, 'but it is
for those for whom it has been prepared by my Father' (Matt. 20:23).

In his letter to the Church at Rome, Paul suggests that predestination is inherent in the teaching of Jesus:

We know that in everything God works for good with those who love
him, who are called according to his purpose. For those whom he
foreknew he also predestined to be conformed to the image of his
Son, in order that he might be the first-born among many brethren.
And those whom he predestined he also called; and those whom he
called he also justified, and those whom he justified he also glorified.
Who shall bring any charge against God's elect? It is God who justi-
fies. (Rom. 8:28–30, 33)

Returning to his Rabbinical training, Paul reflects on God's apparent
capricious action in the lives of the patriarchs, the selection of one son
and the rejection of another, the choice of one people over another
(Israel, not Assyria) and the choice of just a remnant from that chosen
people.

Though the number of the sons of Israel be as the sand of the sea,
only a remnant of them will be saved; for the Lord will execute his
sentence upon the earth with rigour and dispatch. (Rom. 9:27–8)

At the very opening of his letter to the Church at Ephesus, Paul writes:

Blessed be the God and Father of our Lord Jesus Christ, who has
blessed us in Christ with every spiritual blessing in the heavenly

places, even as he chose us in him before the foundation of the world, *that we should be holy and blameless before him.* He destined us in love to be his sons *through Jesus Christ, according to the purpose of his will, to the praise of his glorious grace which will be freely bestowed on us in the Beloved.* (Eph. 1:3–6)

And a tone of predestination permeates the first chapter: 'We who first hoped in Christ have been destined and appointed to live for the praise of his glory.'

A reconciliation of these seemingly predestinarian assumptions in its earliest apologists has produced theological arguments from every corner of the church. There is no single accepted definition of predestination within the Christian churches. For some it is the assumption that an omniscient God has known in advance how individuals would respond to the offer of the gospel and accordingly pre-destined eternal life to those who have responded positively. Others, following Augustine, assume that selection or rejection depends utterly on the good pleasure or will of God, something the church found attractive: salvation was the result of God's grace alone.

So far so good, but what about those who, having lived unquestionably good lives, were not to be so redeemed? Why does God allow some sinners to remain in their sin and then condemn them for it? The doctrine of double predestination (the argument that not only has God predestined those who are to be saved, he has also predestined those who are to be damned) has caused the church even more problems, and theologians from every part of the church have tied themselves in linguistic, philosophical and theological knots trying to explain such apparently unjust, illogical and determinist actions on the part of an all-beneficent, loving God.

Theological determinism is the doctrine that the form of all events is determined according to '*the definite plan and foreknowledge of God*' (Acts 2:23).

But do most Christians today believe that everyone will be saved from hell, won back into relationships of love as John Bowker puts it? Yes, according to Keith Ward of Oxford University:

The most important thing that Christians believe is that God has redeemed everyone from hell. That is to say Christ died, and God in Christ died to reconcile the world to himself. And it is God's desire, as we are told in the New Testament, that everyone without exception should repent and turn to God. So it is God's will that everyone should be redeemed from that state of isolation which is hell. There is a long Christian tradition that those who do not repent will go to hell for ever, but I think that it is clear to a lot of us today that if what Christianity really teaches is that God is absolute unrestricted love; and if what God wants is that everyone should be saved, that is to be brought to love God, then God's wishes are not going to be forever frustrated. I think that most theologians now regret much of the traditional teaching about hell, namely that it is a sort of eternal torture. They would say that hell is where you experience the harm you have done to others, but there is always deliverance from hell. I would think the Christian view when elaborated is a three-stage view.

There is this life, which is a period for learning goodness or learning how we're not good. For some of us it is tragically short and incomplete, and we don't manage to learn those things.

The second is the stage when whatever we've made of our human lives is made clear to us. You might call that hell, heaven, paradise, states of bliss, and states of pain. In both cases they are really brought upon us by our conduct in this life, but it is also a place and a time of learning and development. It is described in the New Testament as a time of sleep – because it is a dream-like state.

And then the Last Judgement when the whole of creation is brought to its consummation. People are faced with that final choice: if any reject – we pray that none do – they are eliminated from the creation. They refuse the love of God. Those who do not reject – and we pray that that is everybody – are taken into the love of God simply by the grace of Jesus Christ. The grace of God working through Jesus Christ will unite them to the divine love for ever, and that third stage is the fulfilment of the universe's purpose in a new creation, in a new heaven and a new earth. So it is a three-stage process: earthly life, intermediate preparatory stage and then the final stage of a new heaven and a new earth described as the city of Jerusalem.

But not all Christians would agree that there will be a chance after death to make good our life on earth – to learn from our past and avoid being judged by our actions and beliefs in this world. For Joel Edwards, the only way to get to heaven is to accept Jesus Christ as a personal Saviour in this life.

> Christian belief in the supremacy of Christ, the total work in the cross and resurrection of Christ as the only way by which people will get to heaven is a very uncomfortable one for most of us, but I think the weight of biblical evidence is quite clear that this is the way God will make an assessment between those who reach the place we call heaven and those who will not. There are very profound questions about those who have never heard the gospel. I am personally satisfied that the scriptures, particularly in places like the letter to the Romans, chapter 1, gives us an understanding that God, who is primarily a God of mercy and a God of love, will assess, will judge those who have never heard the gospel, who have never had the opportunity of hearing about Jesus according to their conscience and the best light they had available to them. But I believe that the Bible is equally clear that those of us who have had the opportunity to hear and respond and for whatever reasons decided that we would not hear and not respond to what Jesus did on the cross, will not respond to the love of God in Christ, will therefore fall in judgement into what the Bible describes as hell.

This position has implications for believers in other religions, other faiths and other ideologies:

> As for people from other faiths, it would seem to me they fall within that category; the likelihood of that being the case is very high. That is one of the prices of the intolerance, if you like, of the gospel. There is that part of the gospel teaching which has become unfashionable. It has become difficult to deal with in a multicultural society, and I believe that the ultimate challenge – and it is a

very serious severe challenge – is that Christians have a primary responsibility to talk about a God of love, not about a God who comes to disqualify Muslims or Hindus or Buddhists or Jews. That is *not* the claim of the gospel. That is *not* the position of the gospel, that is *not* the starting-point and Christians must never be heard even remotely saying or implying that. Our concern is that we speak primarily of a God of love.

But it has to be said that the heart of the Christian gospel leaves us with these difficult and arid possibilities and positions.

While Joel Edwards's position is accepted by many from the evangelical wing of the Christian church, it is one which other Christian theologians cannot accept on intellectual grounds: for example Keith Ward, professor and priest.

I think that is a terrible view, really, although I can see why it exists: people say, 'Well there's no point in being a Christian if you can just get to heaven anyway.' But that is like saying there is no point in making all this effort if God is going to be gracious anyway!

It is true that there are many Christians who think that you will go to hell unless you believe explicitly – in this life – that Jesus is your saviour. Now I think that is totally incompatible with saying that God is a God of love and that God loves everybody and that God wants everybody to be saved. You just cannot believe both those things at the same time! I am quite clear, and it is the declared view of the Roman Catholic Church, that God wills everyone to be saved, that Muslims for example, and all non-Christians, can be saved, and that Christ is the Saviour of everyone, but that does not mean they have to realize it by a specific time in their lives, for example before they're twenty-three.

Who will go to heaven, then, is still a question under discussion for Christians. There's more unity however, on the belief that Christ will come again – perhaps not surprising as the Second Coming, as it's called, is referred to over three hundred times in the New Testament. But what will happen at the second coming and why is it important? Richard Burridge of King's College, London:

What Christians believe about the second coming is that God came in the first coming of Jesus to live among us and share our human lives. In the second coming he will come to answer all the longings of our hearts: for justice to be revealed, for the times of oppression and evil to be brought to an end, for all that is not of God to pass away. We shall live in the love and peace of God. I think for me the end of all things is something I long for and hope for. If we believe in love and truth and justice and honesty and an end to oppression, then surely it is something we should be working towards, which is what it means to belong to the Kingdom of God and be praying for it.

Some Christians, however, believe they know when the Second Coming will be. Over the centuries many dates have been wrongly predicted, and there were no shortage of further predictions as the new millennium approached. John Bowker is dismissive of such crystal-ball-gazing:

Jesus himself said, 'Don't waste time looking for days and seasons. Don't worry about whether it is going to be tomorrow or fifty-five thousand years away. The Kingdom of God is near you already. You become a part of its working out. The Kingdom is already within you.' The Second Coming of Jesus is a way of associating Jesus and keeping Jesus associated with what he has already set in motion: the sovereignty of God can be known and experienced, and must be known and experienced now. If there is going to be a final summing up of all that God purposes and wills at the end of days, Jesus will be there and will be seen to be there. But literal pictures of the Second Coming of Jesus are not important for New Testament faith at all. And if you think of it, it would be slightly absurd if you thought that Jesus was going to come and be here in another body. What is he going to do? Is he going to sift the wheat from the chaff, is he going to walk around and take a bus ride? It becomes absurd. The nearest to a literal picture of a Second Coming of Jesus, that makes sense, is Dostoevsky's picture of the Grand Inquisitor. But the pictures in the New Testament are really not important. The importance is that Jesus is the Kingdom of God in his person.

Whenever, wherever, however the Kingdom of God, the Sovereignty of God, the working out of the purpose and will of God happens, Jesus is there, because Jesus is God. Jesus is the initiative of God, initiating his Kingdom on earth.

It is that understanding of the Kingdom of God that compels Christians to make life here on earth a better place – whether that be working to tackle injustice, poverty or the destruction of the environment, according to Joel Edwards:

A true understanding of heaven and a true understanding of what God expects if we are Kingdom people implicates us in the suffering of our society, implicates us in doing things which change the society in which we live. So Jesus had a mandate to *say* good things and to *do* good things and the church at its best has always done both. It has resisted anything which wants to drive a wedge between the two sides. But the exciting thing is that a proper understanding of heaven, a proper understanding of the future, insists that we become implicated here. And if one looks at passages like Matthew 24 and 25, part of the condition by which people are assessed and judged has to do with how we cared for the poor, how we visited the prisoners, how we looked after the orphans – it is right there in the heart of the gospel. So heaven is about empowerment to be relevant here. And one of the things which excites me as an evangelical Christian is the extent to which increasingly we find a number of churches and Christian groups who are moving to that reality. A good eschatology, a good understanding of future events, locates us powerfully here on earth, so that we don't become so heavenly-minded that we're no earthly use, as the saying goes.

John Bowker spent much of his earlier academic life studying and writing about death in the religions of the world, but as the result of more recent personal experiences he has had the opportunity of anticipating its capriciousness.

What I believe after death is *that God is*, and at that point I can put a full stop. What else do I need to know? I know that God is, partly by looking at the way in which he has transformed the lives of so many people, not just in Judaism or Christianity or Islam, and not just in religions. I know it also from looking at and attending closely to the life of Jesus and all that came from that life immediately in the New Testament writings. I know it in encounter with other people, and I know it more dimly and certainly more incoherently in those moments when I really do know that God has touched my life. I know that God is. And I am not bothered about anything else.

If you ask if I am going to meet my cat in heaven, or am I going to meet grandma in heaven, these are important questions, because life cannot be lived in isolation from others, you can only live in communication and relationship, and you only get to know relationship and communication with particular people, animals, places. Therefore it is absolutely right to ask if I will meet my loved ones in heaven.

It may be that one asks those questions, thinking 'I hope to God not', because relationships are sometimes bleak and full of hate and so on, but we learn relationships not in the abstract but with particular people. Therefore it is important that we ask these questions. What will it be like? Will I meet people I have known?

No one can answer that question. All you can say is that God is. God is in her own nature relationship, communication, love. God has extended that love to us now in creating a world of beauty, of ingenious deviousness, of loveliness. In so many ways the nature of God as creative love has poured out in ways which sometimes seem to us incomprehensible and destructive. It pours out and gathers us up into it, and gathers those whom we love, and all you can say is that gathering cannot possibly cease just because there is a little episode called death. Because of the resurrection we know that death is 'a little episode'. So when I make the claim that I cannot say anything more about life after death than to say that God is, what more *can* I say? God is relationship – that is why we talk about the Communion of Saints.

In a sense you can define a Christian as someone who wakes up each morning and says, 'I am already dead because my life lies hidden with Christ in God'. Now get out of bed and live like that and you are already living after death. You are already living in the

Communion of Saints. I wouldn't worry about anything other than that! You are already in that condition now. How it is to be realized after death, I haven't the slightest idea. Live it now, and because God is, the future will take care of itself.

Index